"With clear text, relatable examples, and useful exercises, [...] tools they need to break free of negative thinking habits a[...] moods. Highly recommended!"

    —**Eileen Kennedy-Moore, PhD**, author of *Raising Emotionally and Socially Healthy Kids*

"In clear language and with accessible, age-appropriate vignettes, Alvord and McGrath do exactly what their title suggests, presenting the nine thinking habits that drag teens down. Better yet, they outline what to do about them with a step-by-step action plan. Easy to read and easy to follow, this immediately useful book will change lives."

    —**Dawn Huebner, PhD**, psychologist and author of the *What-to-Do Guides for Kids*

"Freud based his psychodynamic therapy upon exploring the irrational mind. Beck based cognitive behavioral therapy (CBT) on correcting irrational thoughts. Following Beck, *Conquer Negative Thinking for Teens* by Alvord and McGrath is a clear and practical guide to CBT. This well-written workbook shows teens how to discard distorted thoughts and take control of their own mental health. Informed by years of clinical experience, this book is not just a call-to-reason for adolescents. It will also help parents and professionals think straight and 'keep it real.' A great addition to the CBT literature!"

    —**Daniel G. Shapiro, MD**, developmental and behavioral pediatrics; author of *Parent Child Journey*

"*Conquer Negative Thinking for Teens* gives families the tools to change negative thought patterns that contribute to anxiety, depression, and low self-esteem. It provides relatable examples and fun exercises that give teens control over their thoughts and emotions. Every teenager (and parent of a teen) needs to read this book!"

    —**Kathryn Stamoulis, PhD, LMHC**, therapist and adjunct psychology professor at Hunter College

"Concentrate on the habits that hold you back. Explore other negative habits as you see fit. Diagnose yourself, and then learn to think about your own negative habits differently. And to boot, you will learn some bonus skills such as being mindful of the present moment and putting enjoyable activities in your schedule. This therapeutic strategy of Alvord and McGrath is a no-nonsense, practical approach with very clear steps that a teenager can take to break negative thoughts and habits. The teen gets solid advice based on some very basic principles and procedures of CBT. It is a book I will use with teens and their parents, and it is a book I highly recommend to therapists who work with teens."

> —**K. Daniel O'Leary, PhD**, distinguished professor of psychology at Stony Brook University, and recipient of the APA 2015 Family Psychologist of the Year Award and the 2015 Elizabeth Hurlock Beckman Trust Award for mentoring graduate students

"Great book for any anxious or depressed youth! Mary Alvord has thirty-five years of experience doing CBT with kids and teens. Alvord has distilled the essence of what she does in CBT therapy into this book. Alvord walks a teenager through the process of catching, challenging, and changing the negative thinking habits that make us anxious or depressed. Her engaging style will grab tweens and teens. She does for her reader exactly what a good CBT therapist would do in person. The book is an awesome option for a youth who does not need, cannot find, or would prefer not to see a live CBT therapist. Kids and teens will recognize themselves in Alvord and McGrath's stories, and experience her compassion and gentle, persistent encouragement to alter thinking habits that have made them anxious or depressed. I highly recommend Alvord and McGrath's very readable book for use as a supplement to or alternative to therapy. An important addition to our toolbox!"

> —**Jennifer Lish, PhD**, director of the Worcester Center for Cognitive Behavior Therapy

"Mary Alvord and Anne McGrath's new book, *Conquer Negative Thinking for Teens*, is an exciting new resource for adolescents and their families. This is a practical and highly useful guide for young people who are feeling overwhelmed by negative emotions and thought patterns. Alvord and McGrath provide a clear path for adolescents to recognize common negative thought patterns, and to learn how to overturn those patterns in favor of a more realistic and balanced state of mind. I expect that my patients and their families will really benefit from Alvord and McGrath's straightforward and accessible approach."

> —**Matthew Biel, MD, MSc**, chief of the division of child and adolescent psychiatry at MedStar Georgetown University Hospital, and associate professor of clinical psychiatry and pediatrics at Georgetown University School of Medicine

"This book for teens is written in a manner that displays the authors' ability to connect effectively with teens, comprehensive knowledge of the science pertaining to the treatment of internalizing disorders, and broad and deep experience base collaborating with teens to promote their wellness. I'm confident that teens will find this book to be very relatable and highly practical. Moreover, I believe teens would find that a small investment of their time with this book stands to significantly benefit their day-to-day mental health and wellness. Finally, I believe that clinicians would find that the many practical exercises in this book would synergize their clinical work with teens."

> —**David Palmiter, PhD, ABPP**, author of *Practicing Cognitive Behavioral Therapy with Children and Adolescents* and *Working Parents, Thriving Families*; fellow at the American Psychological Association; past president of the Pennsylvania Psychological Association; and professor of psychology and counseling at Marywood University

"There is no other workbook like this. Concise, thorough, and easy to use, it fills a need felt by clinicians every single day. I plan on giving it to every teen in my practice."

> —**Catherine McCarthy, MD**, child and adolescent psychiatrist in Virginia

conquer negative thinking for teens

a workbook to break the nine thought habits that are holding you back

MARY KARAPETIAN ALVORD, PhD
ANNE MCGRATH, MA

Instant Help Books
An Imprint of New Harbinger Publications, Inc.

Publisher's Note

This publication is designed to provide accurate and authoritative information in regard to the subject matter covered. It is sold with the understanding that the publisher is not engaged in rendering psychological, financial, legal, or other professional services. If expert assistance or counseling is needed, the services of a competent professional should be sought.

Distributed in Canada by Raincoast Books

Copyright © 2017 by Mary Karapetian Alvord and Anne McGrath
               Instant Help Books
               An imprint of New Harbinger Publications, Inc.
               5674 Shattuck Avenue
               Oakland, CA 94609
               www.newharbinger.com

Cover design by Amy Shoup

Acquired by Wendy Millstine

Edited by Gretel Hakanson

All Rights Reserved

Library of Congress Cataloging-in-Publication Data on file

20   19   18

10   9   8   7   6   5   4

To Greg Alvord

And to our children, Bryce, Scott, and Justin

—MKA

In memory of Kevin McManus

And to our children, John and Ellen

—AM

Contents

Introduction   1

1   The "I Can't" Habit   7

2   The Catastrophizing Habit   19

3   The All-or-Nothing Habit   31

4   The Zooming-In-on-the-Negative Habit   43

5   The "I Should, You Should" Habit   57

6   The Fortune-Telling Habit   71

7   The Mind-Reading Habit   83

8   The Blaming Habit   97

9   The "It's Not Fair!" Habit   111

    Acknowledgments   125

    Appendix: A Handy List of Challenge Questions   127

    Resources   131

Introduction

If you're like most teens, you feel some days like you live at the center of a whirlwind of emotions. One minute you're excited and happy, and the next you're sad, anxious, scared, embarrassed, or filled with anger at the outrageously unfair decision that your parents just made. Often, it seems, you're hunkering down in your room by yourself, sad and discouraged. Or fear of looking stupid freezes you in your tracks, preventing you from trying new things. Maybe your anger erupts in sharp and hurtful ways that may feel good in the moment but create conflict in your relationships. Do any of these scenarios sound familiar? It's common to feel helpless when you're swamped with unhappiness and worry or irritation, and to believe that these emotional ups and downs are outside of your control.

But they're not.

What many teens (and lots of adults, too!) don't realize is that we all have the ability to change the course of our emotions. And when we learn how to do that, we also find that we can alter the counterproductive ways we often act as a result of these emotions.

How is it possible to change the way you feel? We're going to let you in on a powerful secret: Your emotions spring directly from your thoughts, and your thoughts do not always reflect the truth. In fact, they're often just plain wrong!

You know that critical voice in your head that often makes you feel terrible ("I'm such a loser!" "I'll never be good enough to make the team!") or mad ("She should have invited me to the party!" "It's not fair that I have a 10:00 p.m. curfew!")? Guess what? You can train your inner critic to turn off that barrage of unfriendly "self-talk" and take a more reasonable, positive tone instead. You'll discover that your self-talk has great power to make you feel terrible. But it also has the potential to make you feel great.

The exercises in this book will teach you how to break nine common negative thinking habits that steer many teens wrong and hold them back from achieving happiness and success. The thoughts that result from these habits are often called "off-target" thoughts, in fact, because our minds accept them as the truth *even when there is absolutely no evidence to support them.*

When teens engage in off-target thinking, as everyone does at times, they're apt to develop a highly distorted view of reality that makes them feel bad. (To get an idea of how distorted thinking can play with the facts, picture fun-house mirrors and how strange they make people look!) Thinking in these faulty ways repeatedly, and becoming convinced that your negative notions are true, can have a significant impact on your outlook and self-esteem. Your fears and doubts can chip away at your willingness to try your hardest and prevent you from experiencing life to the fullest. Your resentment and irritation can get in the way of your relationships with peers and family members. Eventually, these common thinking habits can lead to chronic anxiety and depression. The process that this book takes you through will help you develop more helpful, positive ways of thinking—and the confidence to truly engage in and enjoy your life.

Most teens won't relate to all nine habits. The book is set up in such a way that you can concentrate first on the habits that are holding you back and explore the others as you see fit. The nine thinking errors are described here. Check off the ones that apply to you. (You can also download a copy of this worksheet at http://www.newharbinger .com/38891.)

You may notice strong similarities, and that's okay. Someone who is catastrophizing that disaster will happen in the future is also fortune-telling, for example, but someone who is fortune-telling is not necessarily catastrophizing. Investigate any habits that speak to you!

Nine Thinking Habits

Does it apply?

_____ 1. **The "I can't!" habit.** You automatically conclude that you're not capable of meeting a new challenge or solving a tough problem, which often makes you give up before you even try and feel anxious and sad.

_____ 2. **The catastrophizing habit.** You expect disaster and think *What if …?* whenever you're faced with uncertainty, and you spend a lot of energy feeling needlessly panicky and anxious.

_____ 3. **The all-or-nothing habit.** You see life in extremes. For example, if your performance isn't perfect, it's a total failure. Or any event that doesn't happen one "right" way is all wrong. This makes you feel down on yourself or upset and irritated with others.

_____ 4. **The zooming-in-on-the-negative habit.** You get stuck thinking over and over about your disappointing or embarrassing experiences and filter out everything positive or even just neutral that also happened. Blowing the negative moments way out of proportion results in pessimism about the present and future.

_____ 5. **The "I should, you should" habit.** You hold yourself or other people to a set of rigid and unreasonable rules. When your expectations are not met, you feel disappointed in yourself or frustrated with others.

_____ 6. **The fortune-telling habit.** You jump to the conclusion that you're certainly going to mess up or that a future event will be a disappointment. You tend to either get really down on yourself and feel unmotivated and depressed, or feel cheated and resentful.

_____ 7. **The mind-reading habit.** You jump to the conclusion that someone else is thinking about you and that the thought is critical. This makes you feel unsure of yourself and anxious.

_____ 8. **The blaming habit.** You either think, *It's all my fault!* and feel guilty, or *It's all his fault!* and feel angry and resentful.

_____ 9. **The "It's not fair!" habit.** You get upset when you feel that you've been unjustly treated, even though fairness is an unrealistic expectation.

3

Our purpose in writing this book is to teach you some important skills that will help you turn your negative worldview into a much more balanced and realistic perception of what's going on. The key skill, called "cognitive restructuring," involves a series of steps that help you examine your thoughts for accuracy and develop other possible ways of looking at the situation. Cognitive restructuring works for all of the thinking habits and is practiced in every chapter. There are four steps:

1. First, you catch yourself in your off-target thought as it's going through your head.

2. Next, you consider how the thought makes you want to behave—for example, withdraw to your room or pick a fight with your brother—and how it makes you feel, both physically and emotionally.

3. Then you take a hard look at the evidence and challenge the accuracy of your thought by figuring out what else is more likely true. We call this step a reality check.

4. Finally, you'll come up with a more reasonable and helpful thought based on that more likely truth and a logical and helpful action you can take next as you move forward.

You'll notice as you go through the chapters that brainstorming helpful thoughts and actions—becoming a more realistic, proactive person—are key parts of the game plan. Research on the techniques of a branch of psychology known as cognitive behavior therapy (CBT) has confirmed that our thoughts, moods, and behaviors are all intimately dependent on one another. Your thoughts affect the way you feel and behave, and your behavior can similarly affect your feelings and thoughts. Several giants in the field, notably Aaron Beck and David Burns, are recognized for identifying the common distorted thinking habits you'll tackle in this book and the impact of breaking these habits on your well-being. As you work your way through the book, you'll be called upon to problem solve and push yourself to take action even when you don't want to. This action step can help you experience the pleasure of accomplishment, and that reinforces your new, more helpful thinking pattern. And you'll begin to grasp that effort alone—trying your hardest even though you'll make mistakes—can feel great!

Besides cognitive restructuring, you'll also learn a number of "bonus skills" that add to your habit-breaking toolbox. These skills include such techniques as being mindful of the present moment, showing yourself compassion, putting enjoyable activities into your schedule, and changing your point of view. They are introduced individually in chapters where they can be particularly helpful. But it's worthwhile reading about all of the bonus skills because each one can be applied to breaking any of the habits.

As is true when you try to break any habit, success is clearly going to require hard work and commitment. To get the hang of cognitive restructuring, you have to pay close attention to your thoughts and stick with the practice of these steps. Making changes in life is often a challenge, and it can be scary because change and action often take you outside of your comfort zone. Before you decide to dive right in, it can be helpful to think through why you want to make a change. What do you see as the value of tackling the exercises in this book? Ask yourself: How would my life be better in six months if I could break this thinking habit? How would my relationships improve?

Maybe, for example, your "I can't!" certainty that you're a lousy soccer player is holding you back from joining the recreational league. How much better would life be if you were on a team? Or maybe your habit of mind-reading ("She didn't say hello, so she obviously doesn't like me.") is standing in your way as you try to make new friends. Wouldn't it be great if you were more confident about starting conversations?

The good news is that your commitment is likely to pay off in a big way! The steps of cognitive restructuring, along with the bonus skills, can profoundly change the course you set for yourself as you gain perspective and self-confidence. These skills should serve you well all your life.

chapter 1

The "I Can't" Habit

for you to know

When teens with the "I can't!" thinking habit face a tough problem or have to try something for the first time, they automatically feel scared and helpless and think, *I can't do this!* Rather than looking for small steps they could take to solve a problem or rise to a new challenge, both of which are important to healthy growth and development, they immediately conclude that they don't have any control of the situation. If you have this habit, you may find that you have a tendency to freeze when you think *I can't!* and not take any action at all.

Breaking this thinking habit is important because being unable or unwilling to take action limits your life. Teens who are proactive—meaning they take advantage of the opportunity to try new things and problem solve when sudden obstacles appear in their path—are more resilient people. That means they're better equipped to bounce back from life's disappointments and hurts and accomplish more.

Imagine, for example, that your group history project requires somebody in the group to make a final presentation to the class. Your partners agree that it's your turn since everyone else has already made presentations throughout the semester. You immediately feel panicky and refuse to even consider it, saying, "I can't speak in front of the whole class!" Another member agrees to step up and do the talk, but she's annoyed. Or suppose you would really like to be on the volleyball team. But when the time comes to try out, you think, *I just can't serve the ball!* So you skip tryouts and go home.

The problem with "I can't" thinking is that it can leave you feeling helpless, stuck, anxious, and disappointed in yourself. The problem just gets worse and worse as you lose confidence in your abilities. Eventually, you're likely to become depressed. It's true that often we can't control what's going on around us—if your dad or mom gets a job in a different city, say, you probably aren't going to be able to avoid moving to a new home and a new school. But you almost always have more control than you think in an "I can't!" situation. And even in a case like an unavoidable family move, you can take steps to fit in and be happy at the new school.

The key to breaking the "I can't!" thinking habit is to pause and consider what possible steps you *can* take and then take those steps! Sure, they might be baby steps, but breaking a problem down is a good thing to do. It may help to remind yourself why it's important to you to try—you really love playing volleyball, for example, and being part of the team would be so much fun! It may also help to remember that you've learned and mastered many new skills over the course of your life.

The point is to develop a proactive "I can try this!" attitude, and to practice problem solving so you keep getting better at it. So, for example, rather than thinking, *I can't possibly study everything in time to pass the final!*, you pause, calm down, and then divide the giant study task into daily chunks. You can also ask for help with difficult concepts from your teacher or classmates. Turning to others for help is often a very good way to give yourself the courage to turn an "I can't!" thought into a positive action. Being willing to ask for assistance when it's needed is a key attribute of resilient people.

The payoff to recognizing that you can make a difference in what happens next—and then take action—is that you feel empowered. And that feels good! Life is full of unexpected problems and exciting challenges, and you'll be a much happier, more optimistic person if you believe that you can take steps to meet them.

for you to do

Your goal is to become an "I can try this!" thinker. By practicing a skill called cognitive restructuring, you'll learn to catch yourself when you think *I can't!* and take a reality check: Is it really true that I can't? What's the evidence? What actions am I actually quite able to take? As you work your way through the exercises below, you'll begin to appreciate how much power you have to act, even when you feel scared, and to make a difference in the way your life turns out.

Try It Out: *Cognitive Restructuring*

Every day, Amy meets her friend Brittany for lunch. But Brittany is absent from school today with strep throat and is probably going to have to stay out for a few more days. When Amy gets to the cafeteria and looks for a seat, she spots a group of her classmates laughing and eating together. She wishes she had the nerve to go sit with them but instead thinks: *I'll have to eat alone today. Those girls are all friends, and I can't go over there. They won't want me butting in.*

Amy's off-target thinking error: She believes that there is nothing she can do to make it possible to eat lunch with other classmates. Before she even considers what she might do or say to join the girls, she automatically thinks that she can't figure it out.

What she does (or doesn't do) next as a result of her "I can't!" thought: Amy avoids the girls and sits by herself.

How she feels: She doubts herself and feels anxious about approaching them. This makes her feel sad and lonely.

How her body responds: She tenses up all over, and she frowns.

Reality check: What does Amy say to herself to challenge her off-target thought? She asks herself, "What evidence do I have that those girls would mind having me join them? What makes me think they are unfriendly? I've talked to a couple of them before, and they were nice enough. What are some things I could say to start a conversation?"

Amy's helpful thought and action plan: I really don't want to eat alone again tomorrow, and there are things I can try to avoid it! Tomorrow I'll talk to Sarah after English class and walk to lunch with her. And if that doesn't work, I'll look for someone else to sit with. And this time I'll smile, say hi, and make an effort to be friendly.

The payoff: How do the helpful thought and action plan improve Amy's situation? Though it may be hard for Amy to approach other teens, she feels capable and optimistic when she realizes that there are actions she can take to solve the problem and arrive at her goal: to not eat lunch alone. Figuring out what steps you *can* take in a difficult situation—and then actually putting forth that effort—will give you the confidence that you can make decisions and take actions that will improve your life.

Activity 1: Practice the Steps

David had soccer practice after school and is only turning to his homework at 8:00 p.m. He's hoping his math assignment will be easy because he wants to get online at 9:00. But as soon as he sits down and opens his textbook, he quickly realizes he's in for a long night. He immediately gets really frustrated and thinks, *I can't do this assignment! The formulas are too confusing!*

What was David's off-target thinking error?

_____

_____

What do you think he does (or doesn't do) next as a result of his "I can't!" thought?

_____

_____

♡ How do you think David feels? (Circle all that apply.)

Sad	Disgusted	Calm	Proud
Confused	Annoyed	Grateful	Happy
Angry	Amused	Furious	Lonely
Worried	Helpless	Anxious	Intimidated
Fearful	Stressed	Defeated	Cranky
Frustrated	Upset	Jealous	Misunderstood
Sorry	Tearful	Gloomy	Embarrassed

Other(s): _____

How do you think his body responds? (Circle all that apply.)

Feels shaky	Muscles tense	Heart races	Gets lump in throat
Breathes rapidly	Gets sweaty	Feels cold	Feels tingly
Stomach gets upset	Muscles relax	Gets headache	Feels tired
Neck feels stiff	Mouth feels dry	Feels jittery	Back tenses
Trembles	Feels spacey	Feels dizzy	Fists tighten
Face reddens	Gets fidgety	Feels heavy	Gets stiff

Other(s): _____

✔ Reality check: What can David say to himself to challenge his off-target thought? As soon as he catches himself thinking *I can't do this assignment,* he can question whether that is really true. As he looks for evidence, he asks himself, "Until I try, how do I know I can't do it? Would it help if I read the instructions again? What has happened in the past when I've put effort into learning something new? What can I do to get help if I can't figure out the assignment myself?" Write down what David can say to himself after considering these questions to challenge his off-target thought.

_____

_____

_____

_____

David's helpful thought and action plan: If I take some time and maybe reread the chapter, I'm pretty sure I can figure this out. The teacher wouldn't have assigned it if it's not possible. I can look up the topic online to get ideas and call someone in my class or ask my brother for help if that doesn't work. I can handle it.

The payoff: How do the helpful thought and action plan improve David's situation? Consider the impact on his mood, physical sensations, behavior, and relationships.

_____

_____

_____

_____

Can you see yourself in these "I can't!" examples? Now that you've practiced catching and changing David's thought errors, try the steps out yourself.

Activity 2: Change Your Own Thinking Habit

💭 Remember a time when you were faced with a new challenge or a tough problem and immediately thought, *I can't!* Describe what happened and how your thinking was off-target.

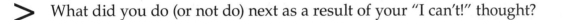

_____

_____

_____

_____

\> What did you do (or not do) next as a result of your "I can't!" thought?

_____

_____

♡ How did this thought make you feel?

_____

_____

 How did your body respond?

_____

_____

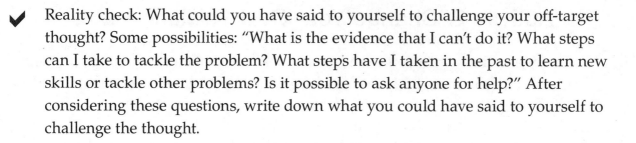 Reality check: What could you have said to yourself to challenge your off-target thought? Some possibilities: "What is the evidence that I can't do it? What steps can I take to tackle the problem? What steps have I taken in the past to learn new skills or tackle other problems? Is it possible to ask anyone for help?" After considering these questions, write down what you could have said to yourself to challenge the thought.

_____

_____

_____

_____

What is a more realistic, helpful thought you might have had instead?

_____

_____

_____

_____

Describe your action plan:

_____

_____

_____

_____

The payoff: How would this helpful thought and action plan have improved your situation? Consider the impact on your mood, physical sensations, behavior, and relationships.

_____

_____

_____

_____

You have the power to silence the "I can't!" messages coming from that voice in your head and brainstorm actions that will let you say "I can try!" Everyone feels scared sometimes to take risks. But always trying to avoid what scares you just keeps you on the sidelines and makes you feel bad. Even taking tiny steps helps build your confidence and feels good.

Try It Out: *Showcase Your Strengths*

Think for a moment about all the things you are good at, and pick your favorite four. Maybe you have a special skill or talent or are a good friend. Perhaps you always try hard to be kind to others. In the boxes below describe or draw pictures or cartoons of your "I can!" actions.

Taking a moment to recognize your strengths is a good way to remind yourself that you're a capable person. That knowledge can give you courage when you're faced with a problem or challenge and your first impulse is to freeze and say, "I can't!"

the big picture on "I can't!" thinking

Believing in your ability to have a say in what happens in your life and to take action that makes a difference is fundamental to being an optimistic and happy person, and a resilient one—somebody who can bounce back with hope from a disappointment or trauma. As we've seen, the opposite is also true: teens who go through life automatically shrinking from challenges and thinking *I can't!* tend to feel anxious, sad, and stuck. In most situations, if you pause to say, "I can try!" you'll discover that you *do* have the power to brainstorm some smart steps to take. Teens who develop the habit of coming up with solutions gradually become more sure of themselves, which adds to their self-esteem. For a practice exercise in "I can try!" thinking, download the "I Can Try!" audio track at http://www.newharbinger.com/38891.

Remember:

- Teens with the "I can't!" habit constantly conclude that they're incapable of meeting a new challenge or solving a tough problem. They tend to freeze helplessly and give up before they even try, becoming anxious and sad or depressed.

- You can train yourself to think *I can try!* instead by looking at the evidence and coming up with an action plan. Ask yourself: What makes me so sure I can't? What are some small steps I can take to make a difference in what happens next?

- Thinking of smart actions to take (and then taking them) is very empowering. Even if you don't feel confident, just try it! With practice, you'll begin to see yourself as a more capable person. And new challenges will seem exciting rather than scary.

chapter 2

The Catastrophizing Habit

for you to know

Have you ever been in a situation where you don't know what's going to happen next, but you're sure that it's going to be horrible? Teens who have the catastrophizing habit automatically imagine the worst possible outcome whenever they face uncertainty, even when there is no reason to expect disaster. This habit is often called "what if?" thinking because as you brace yourself for a catastrophe, you're also picturing what your situation will be like (awful!) when the terrible thing happens. You constantly overestimate the probability of great danger, which leads to panic and ongoing worry.

Suppose your boyfriend or girlfriend goes to spend a week of summer break with family in another state. You send a text one morning to try to stay in touch, but get no response all day. Rather than assuming a misplaced phone or a dead battery, or that your friend is just too busy to chat, your thoughts jump to the worst possible explanation: that he or she doesn't like you anymore and probably has met somebody new. You're so sure that the relationship is over that you can't sleep or think about anything else.

The problem with this habit of anticipating disaster is that it causes you to get stuck in a state of alarm. Our bodies protect us when we face a true danger by pumping out adrenaline and other fight-or-flight chemicals that give us the strength or speed to fight off or escape an angry dog or a burglar, for example. Your heart races, your breathing gets rapid, and your muscles tense as you prepare to spring into action. As your blood is diverted to your muscles and away from your brain and digestive system, you may feel dizzy, light-headed, and like you might vomit. And you may break into a sweat as your body works to cool off.

These responses can be lifesaving when you are truly in danger. But your health and happiness are at risk when this cascade of reactions happens again and again unnecessarily in response to panicky thoughts. In fact, the physical sensations that accompany panic are so unpleasant that some people begin to catastrophize about how their body will react when they face a challenge. "I have to skip school today. It's my turn to give my oral report, and I know I'm going to throw up!" Not surprisingly, the long-term effect of catastrophic thinking is chronic anxiety and a tendency to avoid fear-inducing situations. Also, when you react to a problem or other situation by freezing in fear, your mind isn't able to find solutions or positive actions you might take.

The key to breaking this off-target thinking habit is to catch yourself predicting a terrible event *(Wow, Mom's really mad at Dad! What if they get divorced?)* and take a moment for a reality check. Remind yourself that what your mind is telling you is just a thought and that a thought is not the same as the truth. If you can do that, your racing heart and fast breathing will naturally slow. Then you can begin to brainstorm some other possible (and more likely) outcomes. What has happened before when Mom has been mad at Dad? At the same time, you also remind yourself that you are a capable person, and if something awful really does happen, you have the strength to cope with it.

The payoff of breaking the catastrophizing habit is that your tendency to feel panic lessens. And your overall level of anxiety subsides as you realize that the worst almost never actually happens. Gradually, you gain confidence that what you're facing probably won't be so bad, and even if it is, you can handle it. This more optimistic and balanced outlook helps you stop avoiding events in your life out of fear and gives you courage to take action and try new things.

for you to do

Your goal is to become a "What's most likely true?" thinker. You'll practice recognizing predictions of catastrophe as just thoughts, not reality—and pretty unlikely predictions, at that. The exercises in cognitive restructuring that follow will teach you to catch your off-target thoughts quickly before they cause you to panic. And you'll brainstorm to find more realistic possibilities.

Try It Out: *Cognitive Restructuring*

Abby's sister Catarina was supposed to meet her in the food court at the mall half an hour ago to get pizza and see a movie. But Catarina hasn't shown up yet and isn't responding to Abby's calls and texts. Abby thinks: *Something terrible must have happened! She just got her license. What if she had a bad accident and is hurt?*

Abby's off-target thinking error: She immediately is convinced of the worst possible explanation for her sister's behavior. Abby ignores all of the many possible reasons that people run late and can't get in touch.

What she does (or doesn't do) next as a result of her catastrophizing thought: Abby hurries back and forth from the food court to the nearest parking lot in a panicky way.

How she feels: She is very anxious and agitated.

 How her body responds: Her heart races, and she starts breathing fast. Soon, she feels sweaty, nauseous, and light-headed.

Reality check: What does Abby say to herself to challenge her off-target thought? She reminds herself that she has no idea what is actually holding Catarina up and that there are many possible explanations. She asks herself, "What are some other reasons Catarina might be late? What are the chances that she had a terrible accident? If a friend were in my situation, what advice would I give her? It seems like Catarina would call me if she could, but maybe her phone is dead."

Abby's helpful thought and action plan: Catarina is probably stuck in traffic, and she can't text or call while she's driving! Serious accidents don't happen very often. Let me just take a deep breath to calm down and wait ten more minutes. If I still haven't heard from her, I'll call Mom at work and see what she thinks I should do.

The payoff: How do the helpful thought and action plan improve Abby's situation? Once Abby identifies a less dire (and more likely) explanation for Catarina's failure to show up or call, her panic subsides. So do the unpleasant sensations of a rapid heartbeat, light-headedness, and breathlessness. She can begin to problem solve. Having a plan for what to do next gives her a sense of control, which also helps ease her anxiety. As you'll discover, recognizing catastrophic thoughts for what they are—just thoughts—will go a long way toward helping you approach life with optimism rather than fear.

Activity 1: Practice the Steps

Luke is a good student, but he's had so much homework this week that he's starting to think he hasn't studied enough for a major history test tomorrow. He really wants to ace the test because it'll account for a big chunk of his final grade in the class. And as he starts to think about college and where he might like to apply, he can see that this year's grades will be important. He thinks, *What if I fail this test? I might have to repeat the class! I'm not going to get into college if I blow it.*

What was Luke's off-target thinking error? _____

_____

What do you think Luke does (or doesn't do) next as a result of his catastrophizing thought?

_____

_____

♡ How do you think Luke feels? (Circle all that apply.)

Sad	Disgusted	Confused	Worried
Angry	Amused	Furious	Alone
Helpless	Anxious	Intimidated	Fearful
Irritable	Comfortable	Distressed	Uncomfortable
Gloomy	Energized	Embarrassed	Sorry
Tearful	Shaky	Panicked	Scared
Disappointed	Hurt	Misunderstood	Neutral

Other(s): _____

👤 How do you think his body responds? (Circle all that apply.)

Feels shaky	Muscles tense	Heart races	Gets lump in throat
Breathes rapidly	Feels sluggish	Gets sweaty	Feels cold
Hands get clammy	Feels nauseous	Feels dizzy	Jaw clenches
Stomach gets upset	Muscles relax	Frowns	Gets headache
Feels energetic	Face reddens	Gets fidgety	Feels spacey
Gets stomach cramps	Face scrunches up	Fists clench	Mouth feels dry

Other(s): _____

✔ Reality check: What can Luke say to himself to challenge his off-target thought? Luke can think about his previous performance and ask himself: "How many times have I failed a history test? How likely is it, based on what I know of the material, that I will fail this time? Plus, I can make time to study tonight." In the same way, he can ask himself how likely it is that he would have to repeat the class or miss out on college even if he does blow the test. Write down what Luke can say to himself after considering these questions to challenge his off-target thought.

_____

_____

_____

_____

Luke's helpful thought and action plan: I've learned most of the material already, and I usually do well on tests. I'll make sure I review everything again and get a lot of sleep tonight! Even if I do get a low grade on this test, I have lots of time to bring all of my grades up before applying to college. I'll keep studying hard and do my best, and I'll get into a good school.

The payoff: How do the helpful thought and action plan improve Luke's situation? Consider the impact on his mood, physical sensations, behavior, and relationships.

_____

_____

_____

_____

Do you often find yourself in a panic and braced for disaster? Try taking these steps yourself.

Activity 2: Change Your Own Thinking Habit

Remember a time when you automatically catastrophized that something terrible was bound to happen. Describe the circumstances and how your thinking was off-target.

_____

_____

_____

_____

> What did you do (or not do) next as a result of your catastrophizing thought?

_____

_____

♡ How did this thought make you feel?

_____

_____

☗ How did your body respond?

_____

_____

✔ Reality check: What could you have said to yourself to challenge your off-target thought? Some possibilities: "How likely is the worst-case scenario? Is there any evidence that it's apt to happen? What are five other things more likely to happen? If something bad does happen, how could I cope? What would I tell a friend who had the same thought?" After considering these questions, write down what you could have said to yourself to challenge the thought.

_____

_____

_____

_____

☁ What is a more realistic and helpful thought you might have had instead?

_____

_____

_____

_____

🚶 Describe your action plan:

_____

_____

_____

_____

The payoff: How would this helpful thought and action plan have improved your situation? Consider the impact on your mood, physical sensations, behavior, and relationships.

_____

_____

_____

_____

Clearly, there's a big benefit in breaking the habit of expecting catastrophe! You want to practice redirecting your thinking toward more realistic alternatives as soon as you catch yourself predicting disaster and before panic kicks in. Mastering this ability will save you a huge amount of needless anxiety and give you a much more upbeat, healthy outlook on what lies ahead.

Try It Out: *Get Real!*

Read each example of off-target catastrophizing in the left-hand column on the next page. Challenge it by asking yourself how likely it is to happen. Think about what you might tell a friend who was having this thought. Then draw a line to match the thought with a more helpful, realistic thought from the other column.

Off-Target Thoughts	Helpful Thoughts
	The doors are locked. I can either stay awake and worry, or I can choose to sleep knowing that it's not likely to happen.
What if I fail the science test?	
	I usually only throw up if I am very sick. Even if I do, what's the worst thing that will happen?
What if I forget all my lines in the play?	
	My eyes are probably just tired.
What if there is a break-in while we're sleeping?	
	I will organize my time so I can fit the work in. If I need to, I will get up earlier the next morning.
My friend says she can't come over. What if she doesn't want to be friends anymore?	
	I will study and ask about anything I don't understand.
I have a headache. What if it's a brain tumor?	
What if I throw up in class?	She must already have plans today.
	I already know the part well, and I did fine at the dress rehearsal.
What if I can't get all my work done?	

It's natural to worry a little when you're faced with uncertainty. But as this exercise illustrates, the worst-case scenario is rarely very likely to occur. In your own life, that becomes clear as you practice listing the many more-probable possibilities. As you focus on the possibilities that are realistic, you feel much calmer and more hopeful.

the big picture on catastrophizing

The habit of believing the worst is bound to happen results in needless panic and worry and eventually to chronic anxiety. Blowing the danger out of proportion also tends to make you retreat from problems or challenges rather than thinking up creative ways to meet them head on. The idea is to interrupt this process and practice reading situations more accurately, which allows you to react in an effective way instead of with panic. Sometimes, of course, bad things do happen, and your fears will be justified. So it is important to remind yourself that, should disaster strike, you have the strength and the smarts to figure out how to cope.

Remember:

- Teens with the catastrophizing habit automatically expect disaster when they're faced with uncertainty and spend a lot of energy feeling needlessly panicky and anxious.

- You can break this habit by taking a reality check. Ask yourself: "Is disaster really probable? What are five other possibilities more likely to happen?"

- When you stop responding to every uncertainty or challenge with great alarm or gloom, you feel calmer and are able to problem solve. And you feel more confident about taking risks and testing your limits.

chapter 3

The All-or-Nothing Habit

for you to know

Imagine that you are auditioning for a part in the school play and you stumble over your lines. Or that your soccer teammate passes you the ball and it whizzes right past you to a player on the other team. It's only natural to be disappointed when such missteps occur. But ideally we are able to see them as the temporary ups and downs that everybody encounters in daily life and just resolve to do better next time.

But teens who are prone to the all-or-nothing thinking habit have a perspective on the world that allows only black-or-white extremes. So when their performance is not absolutely perfect, they see it as a total failure. Or when bad weather means a beach trip has to be postponed, a whole day of summer is completely wasted. Instead of looking at a situation and seeing a whole spectrum of possibilities that exist, they immediately conclude, "I'm such a loser!" or "Now my day is ruined!"

These examples illustrate two types of all-or-nothing thinking: expecting only perfection of yourself and expecting other people to do exactly what you think is correct or events to happen in only one "right" way with no options in between.

The problem with being a perfectionist is that perfection is rarely possible. Pursuing it at all costs has the effect that "good" or even "great" brings no satisfaction or joy. And any failure, which is a natural part of growing and stretching, is absolutely unacceptable. Of course, it's healthy and admirable to strive to do your best. But everyone makes mistakes! And the reality is that an 85 or 90 percent on a chemistry test is far from a failure. Teens who always set an unrealistically high bar for themselves are very likely to lose confidence in their abilities. Their self-esteem falters because it's usually impossible to clear the bar. They are apt to be fearful of trying new things and may be troubled by chronic anxiety and depression.

A second type of all-or-nothing thinking allows for other people to act in only one "right" way or sees only one possible outcome in any given situation. "I know the right rules to this game! If she has a different way of keeping score, she's wrong!" you might say to yourself. Teens who think this way often come across to friends and family as supercritical, stubborn, or uncompromising and unable to see other points of view. Such rigid thinkers have a tendency to be angry and resentful a lot—and to have other people mad at them, too. And because they can't easily see that there are alternatives, they have a tough time generating creative ways to solve problems and negotiate solutions.

The key to breaking the all-or-nothing thinking habit is to catch yourself in the act and pause to think about the many possible ways that events can unfold in between "fantastic" and "completely terrible." To get the idea, consider the extremes of hot and cold. Imagine the many degrees of temperature between freezing and boiling. The spectrum of possibilities in life is similar. Whenever you feel absolutely positive that you've just experienced a huge failure, try to imagine the whole range of what else might be true instead. Maybe your party didn't go perfectly (some people showed up late, and your dad told an embarrassing joke). But for the most part, people had fun!

The payoff to seeing and accepting that lots of possibilities exist—and that many of them are good or at least okay possibilities—is that you begin to put your ups and downs in perspective. You are bound to feel a whole lot happier if you can allow yourself to goof up occasionally as a normal part of practicing and getting better. And you'll be increasingly confident about your ability to take the risks we all must take as part of growing up, trying new things, and forming new relationships. Friendships will be much easier to sustain when you can react flexibly to the unexpected ways other people act. And teens who are open and welcoming to the multiple alternatives between right and wrong, for example, tend to be more content and more resilient.

What if you do sometimes mess up in a big way? Failure is often a wonderful opportunity for growth. Sometimes it's even the reason that new discoveries happen. It's well established in business and sports, for example, that trial and error—and sometimes striking out completely—is a very good way to learn, figure out what works, and eventually succeed.

for you to do

Your goal is to become a "let's look at all the points on the spectrum" thinker. Using the skill of cognitive restructuring, your aim is to practice noticing the wide range of possibilities that exist between two extreme ways of seeing a situation. Taking a reality check will help you challenge thoughts that reflect an all-or-nothing view of the world by coming up with a list of other in-between descriptions of what might be true. With that information, you can arrive at a more helpful way of thinking and reacting.

Try It Out: *Cognitive Restructuring*

Kamal is spending the afternoon shopping for soccer cleats at the mall. When he walks through the food court, he spots three of his teammates having pizza and laughing loudly several tables away. He calls out hello as he passes by, but nobody responds. Kamal immediately thinks, *They don't like me. I'll never have friends on the team.*

☁ **Kamal's off-target thinking error:** He sees no in-between possibilities that might explain why his teammates didn't at least wave back or maybe even wave him over to their table. Kamal interprets their simple lack of response, which might be caused by other things, to mean that he is not liked.

\> **What he does (or doesn't do) next as a result of his all-or-nothing thought:** Kamal doesn't call out again or go over to the table. He just walks away.

♡ **How he feels:** He feels dismissed and invisible—and sad about it.

🧍 **How his body responds:** He feels a lump in his throat and a tightness in his chest.

✔ **Reality check: How does Kamal examine and challenge his off-target thought?** He asks himself, "What are other possible reasons the guys didn't say anything? I wonder if they didn't hear or see me. How do they normally treat me?"

Kamal's helpful thought and action plan: The food court is really crowded and noisy, so that probably explains it. Besides, at practice nobody ignores me. Next time I see some guys outside of school, I'll go right up to them to say hello instead of avoiding them.

The payoff: How do the helpful thought and action plan improve Kamal's situation? His mood improves, and his body relaxes when he stops seeing his teammates' lack of attention as unfriendliness directed at him. When he sees the guys again, he doesn't hesitate to approach them and join the conversation. For you, too, the ability to see the whole range of possibilities and react to other people realistically is a key step in making and keeping friends.

Activity 1: Practice the Steps

Isabella stands in front of the class to present her part of a group science project. Partway through she loses her place in the notes and freezes for a few seconds in panic. She stumbles through the rest of her report and rushes to her seat thinking, *I blew it, so my group is going to get a failing grade because of me!*

What was Isabella's off-target thinking error?

_____

_____

What do you think Isabella does (or doesn't do) next as a result of her all-or-nothing thought?

_____

_____

♡ How do you think Isabella feels? (Circle all that apply.)

Disgusted	Calm	Sad	Confused
Annoyed	Embarrassed	Angry	Amused
Lonely	Fearful	Stressed	Irritable
Helpless	Anxious	Intimidated	Discouraged
Distressed	Uncomfortable	Tearful	Gloomy
Shaky	Panicked	Scared	Hopeless
Lost	Rejected	Disappointed	Frustrated

Other(s): _____

🧍 How do you think her body responds? (Circle all that apply.)

Muscles tense	Heart races	Feels lump in throat	Frowns
Breathes rapidly	Gets sweaty	Feels listless	Feels cold
Feels dizzy	Face reddens	Hands clench	Stomach tightens
Stomach gets upset	Gets headache	Feels heavy	Mouth feels dry
Stiffens	Face tightens	Eyes roll	Shoulders slump
Jaw tightens	Feels numb	Skin feels tingly	Feels hot

Other(s): _____

✔ Reality check: What can Isabella say to herself to challenge her off-target thought? She asks herself: "Am I really likely to cause a failing grade for the whole group? Even though I stumbled, I had good information. Am I thinking in extremes? Have others made mistakes while speaking? What happened in their case?" Write down what Isabella can say to herself after considering these questions to challenge her off-target thought.

_____

_____

_____

_____

 Isabella's helpful thought and action plan: I worked really hard on my report. Even though it wasn't perfect, I kept going and did a pretty good job. I've watched speakers stumble before, and it didn't bother anyone. Next time I have to present a report, I'll practice in front of the mirror to try to do my best. And, if I make a mistake, I'll remember that doing my best can be good enough.

The payoff: How do the helpful thought and action plan improve Isabella's situation? Consider the impact on her mood, physical sensations, behavior, and relationships.

_____

_____

_____

_____

Now that you've watched Kamal and Isabella look at the many possibilities between their own extremes, try taking the wider view yourself.

Activity 2: Change Your Own Thinking Habit

 Can you remember a time when you were an all-or-nothing thinker? Perhaps you were in a situation where you felt your performance had to be perfect, and when you made a mistake, you thought, *I'm such a failure!* Maybe you messed up on a math test once and thought, *I'm never going to be good at math.* Describe what happened and your extreme thought.

_____

_____

_____

_____

> What did you do (or not do) next as a result of your all-or-nothing thought?

_____

_____

 How did that thought make you feel?

_____

_____

♟ How did your body respond?

_____

_____

✔ Reality check: What could you have said to yourself to challenge your off-target thought? Some possibilities: "Is my thought at one extreme? Is there evidence to support my thought? Is there evidence against it? What are some possibilities that fall in between the extremes?" After considering these questions, write down what you could have said to yourself to challenge the thought.

_____

_____

_____

_____

What is a more realistic, helpful thought you might have had instead?

_____

_____

_____

_____

🚶 Describe your action plan:

_____

_____

_____

_____

The payoff: How would this helpful thought and action plan have improved your situation? Consider the impact on your mood, physical sensations, behavior, and relationships.

_____

_____

_____

_____

While it's commendable to want to do your best, remember that no one can achieve perfection, and that trying and stumbling and trying again is the way we all learn and grow! Being accepting of yourself when you trip up is important to your self-esteem and your willingness to get back in the game and try again. And being accepting of others when events play out differently than you expect is key to having good relationships with friends and family.

Try It Out: _Widen Your Lens_

Remember that even a single color can be found in a seemingly endless number of different shades. Pick one color, such as blue or green. Go outside (or look out the window) and count all the shades of the color that you can see.

It's important to keep in mind that this is the way life works too. Most of the time when you make a mistake or face a situation that seems bitterly disappointing and absolutely terrible, there are actually many, many ways of looking at that reality in between the extremes.

more for you to do

Learn a Bonus Skill: *Get Comfortable with Discomfort*

The common feeling that arises from many thinking errors is severe discomfort. You may be fearful and anxious, for example, or angry and resentful when people don't act the way you feel is correct. Physically, you may be so worried about getting nauseous that you avoid activities. When you are a perfectionist, for example, you feel very uncomfortable when you make mistakes, and this fear of failure can cause you to avoid trying anything new.

One way to tackle this problem is to take a risk and intentionally expose yourself to the troubling emotions and sensations. The goal is to get accustomed to simply letting them be. Getting better at tolerating discomfort allows you to be braver about trying things and more open to the wide range of possibilities that really exists.

Try It Out!

To get comfortable with uncomfortable emotions and sensations, think of a time when you made an embarrassing mistake, were very worried, or were upset that a friend did something "wrong." Jot down the situation in the space below. Now close your eyes and put yourself back in that moment. Try reliving the feelings you experienced at the time, one by one, in all of their intensity. On a scale of zero to ten (with ten being the highest), rate your level of discomfort. Imagine and stay with those feelings for as long as it takes to begin to get used to the feelings and to tolerate them better. You'll notice that your level of discomfort ratchets down. Make a note of your final level. You'll be surprised how this exercise can help you get comfortable with discomfort.

Situation: _____

_____

_____

_____

Feeling	Initial Discomfort Level (0–10)	Final Discomfort Level (0–10)

The downside of letting your fears and resentments overwhelm you is that you avoid experiences and struggle in your relationships. This exercise will remind you that you have the power to tolerate difficult feelings and not let them get in your way.

the big picture on all-or-nothing thinking

Any given event can develop in dozens of different ways, and many—even if not your first choice—are just fine. If you're not making a mistake every so often, the chances are good that you're not trying fun new things and taking some risks to test your capabilities. You're bound to be happier and more confident when you understand that there are degrees of success. And when you can react flexibly and with good humor to what other people say or do, you'll get more enjoyment out of your friendships!

Remember:

- Teens who have the all-or-nothing habit think in extremes. They might be perfectionists, not allowing themselves any leeway to make mistakes, or they may believe that any event that doesn't happen their one "right" way is all wrong. They often are down on themselves or upset and irritated at others.

- You can break this habit by taking a reality check. Ask yourself: "Am I thinking in extremes? Are there other in-between possibilities that would actually be fine or good enough?"

- Breaking this habit helps you become more open to the unexpected and less afraid of making mistakes. As you become more flexible, your self-confidence grows, you're easier to get along with, and you experience more joy.

chapter 4

The Zooming-In-on-the-Negative Habit

for you to know

Your brain is designed to be an excellent filter, allowing you to pay close attention to what's important in the moment while ignoring the constant bombardment of other information coming in. That's why you can cram for an afternoon math test in a noisy cafeteria or concentrate on texting with a friend while everyone in your family is talking at once.

But sometimes that filtering action (also known as "selective attention") gives you a badly distorted perception of reality. When you have this off-target thinking habit, your attention zooms in on a negative event or two as the day goes on and you get stuck thinking about the bad stuff. You can't see the big picture, which is also composed of hundreds of other moments in your day that were interesting, exciting, fun, or even just okay. As a result, disappointments are blown way out of proportion, and your accomplishments and pleasures get lost.

Suppose your history teacher makes a sarcastic comment one day in class when you raise your hand and get the definition of "absolute monarchy" wrong. If you have the zooming-in-on-the-negative habit, you can't stop thinking about it. You filter out of your awareness the goal you scored in P.E. class and the fun you had walking home from school with a friend. You think, *My teacher was really mean! This was really a terrible day!* A related problem when you have this habit is that your memory of events is also skewed. So even many days later, the disappointment or embarrassing moment may run on an endless loop in your mind, overwhelming any memories of events that led to any feelings of happiness or pride or satisfaction.

Paying attention selectively to the disappointing occurrences in your life while filtering out everything else makes you feel bad about yourself or others and pessimistic about your future. Or it makes you resentful and angry that life just isn't going your way. Over time, this habit of psychological inflexibility, of taking account of only the negative details, can lead you to withdraw from other people and activities and to eventually get sad or depressed.

The key to breaking the habit is to catch yourself when you zoom in on a negative incident that takes all your attention. Sometimes really sad things are going to happen, and thinking about them is a normal part of processing them and moving forward. Plus, if you do make a mistake, you want to learn from it, not ignore it. But the idea is to interrupt that endless loop of negative self-talk and turn off the filter that causes you to ignore everything else going on in your life. You're aiming for a realistic and appropriately balanced understanding of the big picture. In other words, you'll try to capture all the "ups" and the "okays" that have happened along with the "downs."

One of the best effects of breaking this habit is that, as you begin to pay attention to the positive and so-so aspects of your life, you feel more content and more hopeful. By taking in the big picture rather than zooming in on one small piece of it, you're able to see that your disappointments aren't so overwhelming. As you start enjoying (and remembering) the many satisfying moments that make up a normal day, you look forward to joining in the fun with your friends.

for you to do

Your goal is to become a "let's look at the big picture" thinker. The steps of the cognitive restructuring process will help you get used to stepping back and taking in the whole. You will learn to notice all of the good and the average moments in life along with the not-so-good moments. You'll do this by taking a reality check and looking at the evidence that your negative thinking represents the entire story. Finally, you'll learn how to come up with a more balanced and accurate view of the situation and a plan of action that is in sync with that view.

Try It Out: *Cognitive Restructuring*

Tyler's ninth-grade basketball team has had a great season so far. He feels especially excited going into Thursday's game because he's been doing really well in practice and he thinks he will get a chance to start. That doesn't happen. But Tyler does get to play the whole second half and makes a great pass that results in a basket. And his team wins. Rather than enjoying his and his teammates' successes, however, he thinks: *I'm just not good enough to ever start the game! My life is terrible!* He feels really glum and skips pizza with the team after the game.

💭 **Tyler's off-target thinking error:** He filters out all of the good things that happened during the game—his time on the court, his great play, the team's win—as well as the many other moments of enjoyment he had during the day. Instead, he selectively focuses on his one disappointment.

❯ **What he does (or doesn't do) next as a result of his zooming-in-on-the-negative thought:** Tyler gets out of the locker room as fast as possible and heads home. He misses out on the team's celebration.

♡ **How he feels:** He feels irritated, down, and discouraged.

🧍 **How his body responds:** His shoulders are tense, his stomach feels queasy, and he lacks energy.

✔ **Reality check: What does Tyler say to himself to challenge his off-target thought?** Tyler looks for evidence that he's a poor player and that his life is terrible. He challenges that thought by saying to himself: "Too bad that I didn't get to start. But let's look at the big picture. I did get to play a lot, and we won! What went well during the game? What else happened today that was good?"

🏃 **Tyler's helpful thought and action plan:** I really like playing basketball, and I am lucky to be on the team. It gives me a chance to hang out with my friends and get better at a sport. I have a choice of what to focus on. I will keep practicing as hard as I can, and maybe someday I will get to start.

🎖 **The payoff: How do the helpful thought and action plan improve Tyler's situation?** Seeing the big picture reminds Tyler that one disappointment doesn't really take away from how much he enjoys practicing and playing basketball and how much it means to him being part of the team. In fact, he sees his disappointment instead as a reason to practice harder. Having this plan makes him optimistic that he can improve his game. By changing your perspective to get a fuller picture when you zoom in on a negative, you, too, will soon see that you've almost certainly blown it way out of proportion. Your mood will improve, and you'll feel motivated to get back into action.

Activity 1: Practice the Steps

Layla has had a pretty interesting few days. She made $35 taking care of her favorite neighborhood puppy, and she was invited to go to the movies with three girls from school this weekend. On Wednesday, though, she found out that she got a D on her English literature test. Since then, that grade is all Layla can think about. She tells herself: "I had a really bad week."

💭 What was Layla's off-target thinking error?

_____

_____

> What do you think Layla does (or doesn't do) next as a result of her zooming-in-on-the-negative thought?

_____

_____

♡ How do you think Layla feels? (Circle all that apply.)

Hurt	Enraged	Furious	Misunderstood
Sad	Disgusted	Confused	Annoyed
Worried	Rejected	Vulnerable	Alone
Helpless	Anxious	Intimidated	Stressed
Satisfied	Irritable	Distressed	Gloomy
Uncomfortable	Defeated	Tearful	Shaky
Hopeless	Scared	Disappointed	Frustrated

Other(s): _____

How do you think her body responds? (Circle all that apply.)

Feels shaky	Legs tense	Heart races	Feels heavy
Throat tightens	Breathes rapidly	Feels tired	Hands clench
Skin feels clammy	Face feels hot	Feels energetic	Feels sweaty
Feels cold	Muscles relax	Frowns	Body stiffens
Stomach gets upset	Feels numb	Gets headache	Feels weak
Feels jittery	Shoulders slump	Head drops	Feels breathless

Other(s): _____

_____

Reality check: What can Layla say to herself to challenge her off-target thought? When Layla examines the evidence that she had a really bad week, what does she notice? She asks herself, "Am I looking at the whole week, or one small part? What else happened this week? What went well?" Write down what Layla can say to herself after considering these questions to challenge her off-target thought.

_____

_____

_____

_____

Layla's helpful thought and action plan: It's too bad that I got a bad grade, but it was only one test and I know I can do better. I'll ask my teacher if I can do anything for extra credit and study harder next time. I can always ask for help if there's something I don't understand.

The payoff: How do the helpful thought and action plan improve Layla's situation? Consider the impact on her mood, physical sensations, behavior, and relationships.

_____

_____

_____

_____

Now that you've learned how to broaden your perspective, noticing the good and the okay as well as the awful, try taking these steps yourself.

Activity 2: Change Your Own Thinking Habit

Think of a time when you zoomed in on a negative experience and blew it way out of proportion. Describe what happened and how your thought about that day or week was off-target.

_____

_____

_____

_____

> What did you do (or not do) next as a result of your zooming-in-on-the negative thought?

_____

_____

_____

_____

♡ How did this thought make you feel?

_____

_____

♦ How did your body respond?

_____

_____

✔ Reality check: What could you have said to yourself to challenge your off-target thought? Some possibilities: "Is there evidence to support my thought? Is there evidence against it? Am I focusing too much on one detail? What good things happened that I'm forgetting? Next week, when I think back on today, what would be the most accurate way to remember the big picture?" After considering these questions, write down what you could have said to yourself to challenge the thought.

_____

_____

_____

_____

What is a more realistic, helpful thought you might have had instead?

_____

_____

_____

_____

Describe your action plan:

_____

_____

_____

_____

The payoff: How would this helpful thought and action plan have improved your situation? Consider the impact on your mood, physical sensations, behavior, and relationships.

_____

_____

_____

_____

It's amazing how different a picture looks when you step back and view it as a whole! In effect, that's what your reality check will prompt you to do whenever you catch yourself overwhelmed by upsetting events. Getting that balanced perspective, and learning to recognize and appreciate what's going on that's positive, will help you cope with disappointment without losing your optimism and sense of possibility.

Try It Out: *Shift Your Focus*

Make a list of ten things that happened in your life this week. Try to come up with several that were good, a few that were disappointing, and some that were just so-so.

1. _____

2. _____

3. _____

4. _____

5. _____

6. _____

7. _____

8. _____

9. _____

10. _____

It's clear that zooming in on a negative experience can make you sad. What would happen if you were to zoom in on a great experience? Choose the event from your list above that makes you proudest or happiest, and experiment with zooming in on it, minimizing all the other experiences. Describe how zooming in on the positive makes you feel.

_____

_____

_____

_____

Of course, focusing only on the positive part of that picture will also give you a distorted view of the whole. But it feels good, doesn't it? Trying this exercise every once in a while is a great way to remind yourself of how this thought habit works, and of how powerful your thoughts are in affecting your feelings, your body sensations, and your actions.

more for you to do

Learn a Bonus Skill: *Get Moving!*

Often when negative thoughts cause you to feel really down on yourself or mad at other people, you get into a cycle of avoiding situations and withdrawing from social activities, which makes you feel even worse. Practicing the skill of behavioral activation—in other words, just doing something even when you don't want to— slowly brings back into your life activities that are important to you and make you feel better emotionally and physically. Sometimes we think of behavioral activation as changing thoughts by working in reverse, or from the "outside" to the "inside." In other words, as a first step we go out and do something that we may not feel like doing, and that action makes us feel better and gives us more positive energy.

Start by listing some activities you like (or used to like). Then schedule them into your day or week. You might feel so down that you'd rather listen to music in your room than go to the homecoming game, for example. But forcing yourself to go anyway and smile and talk with your friends makes you feel less down and gets you out of your funk. This leaves you more likely to think realistic, optimistic thoughts.

Try It Out!

To try behavioral activation, think of several activities that you enjoy and think are important, such as playing a sport, going to the movies, or hanging out with your friends. Schedule at least two or three of these enjoyable and important experiences into the week ahead so you get up and engage in life even when you're feeling down and would rather not. Note how each activity affects your mood and what you think afterward.

Behavioral Activation Scheduling

Day and Time	Activity	Mood	Thoughts

The feelings of depression that result from all sorts of off-target thinking patterns are sometimes so strong that you lack any motivation to be friendly and sociable. You may not even have enough energy to take a reality check and try to change those thought patterns. At times like these, a dose or two of behavioral activation can be just what you need to ignite positive feelings and get you engaged in life again. It can be hard to take action, but it does get easier once you get moving.

the big picture on zooming in on the negative

Whenever your mind gets stuck on a disappointment or an embarrassing moment, remember that you're focusing on just one small part of a much bigger picture. You have the power to pause and zoom out. This allows you to see and appreciate the many other details you've been missing. Gaining this more balanced view will help you put those disappointments in perspective.

Remember:

- Teens with the zooming-in-on-the-negative habit get stuck on their disappointing or embarrassing experiences. They think about them over and over as they filter out the many positive or neutral events that also happened. Blowing those negative moments way out of proportion results in pessimism about the present and future.

- You can break this habit by taking a reality check. Ask yourself: "Am I focused just on a single detail or two of my day or week? What else happened that was good or just okay?"

- When you look at the big picture, those negatives shrink to their proper size alongside all the positives. You begin to appreciate what's good in your life and feel happier and more optimistic.

chapter 5

The "I Should, You Should" Habit

for you to know

Teens who have the "I should, you should" thinking habit constantly hold themselves and their parents and friends to a rigid set of rules about how they should behave. Sometimes, of course, you do need to act in a certain way. For example, it's reasonable to think, *I really have to study hard for my test tomorrow,* or *We should go easier on the substitute teacher!*

But when teens set unrealistic bars for themselves to meet—or impose expectations on others—they frequently are disappointed, hurt, or angry when those expectations aren't met. They completely miss that other possible behaviors or outcomes are actually more reasonable and perfectly acceptable.

If you're an "I should" thinker, you might get really disgusted with yourself after hitting a wrong note playing your trumpet at a school band concert, for example. You might think, *I should always play my part without making any mistakes!* Or you might feel so awkward at a party that you're afraid to make conversation, and come home thinking, *I should be funnier!* Such rigid thinking doesn't take into account that everyone makes mistakes. Or that being yourself is just fine.

Or if you tend to be a "he should" or "they should" thinker, you might regularly feel hurt or get irritated with your friends. You might think, for example, *She should have done a lot more for my birthday,* or *He should respond right away when I text him.* The problem here is that you're ignoring the reality that your friends are focused on their own lives. Their choices may very well be different from the choices you would like them to make. And that's okay. There is almost always a whole range of ways that any situation can develop. And there may be perfectly fine reasons for all of them!

Sometimes, the problem is that you set rules for the way the world should work, regardless of what is actually realistic. For example: True friends shouldn't have arguments. Teachers should never give homework on the weekends.

Getting stuck in such inflexible thinking patterns often leads to feelings of guilt, regret, betrayal, disappointment, depression, and anger. When you apply such rules to your own actions and don't measure up, you are likely to feel that you have messed up or let others down. This may make you start to withdraw. When you hold other people responsible for acting a certain way, their failure to do what you want may make you angry and resentful. As a result, you may reject them—or they may start avoiding you.

The key to breaking this thinking habit is to take a hard look at your "shoulds" and "musts" and learn to identify which ones are actually your wants and desires and which expectations are sensible and helpful. When common sense tells you a "should" statement is reasonable (for example, "He shouldn't be driving alone since he only has his learner's permit"), meeting that standard may be important. On the other hand, when you examine a "should" statement and realize that it is just a reflection of your own preferences, it's smart to imagine other possibilities. And try substituting a more flexible thought instead, such as *It would be nice if …* or *I'd prefer that …* or *It would be helpful if …* Remember that many different outcomes can be just fine!

The payoff of breaking this thinking habit is that you can begin to be glad about (or at least okay with) what is actually going on in the present. You stop being angry or sad that things aren't different. That allows you to be more accepting of yourself and others and just more flexible in general. And that makes you a lot easier to get along with. Being more forgiving of your own actions eases those feelings of guilt, which so frequently lead to depression. Plus, being more relaxed about the way things go should improve your relationships with your friends and family members—which will go a long way toward making you happier.

for you to do

Your goal is to become an "It would be nice if … " thinker. By catching yourself in rigid "should" statements, and examining and challenging them, you can begin to get away from constant rule-setting. You'll ask yourself how realistic a "should" thought is and consider what other possibilities are more reasonable. You'll get the hang of recognizing which "shoulds" are actually just your own personal preferences. As a result, you'll become more open to letting things happen in ways that are not *your* way.

Try It Out: *Cognitive Restructuring*

Kayla needs to be at school by 10:00 a.m. on Saturday for track practice. She's excited to be driving herself since she's only had her license for a week. Unfortunately, a big traffic tie-up halfway to school causes her to run ten minutes late. She immediately feels disappointed in herself and embarrassed for not meeting her responsibilities. "I should never be late!" she chastises herself. The practice has started by the time she gets to the track, and the coach gives her a questioning look. She starts running sprints, but her times are off, and her "I should" thinking leaves her feeling down.

Kayla's off-target thinking error: While in general it's good to be on time for practices, in this case, Kayla's inflexible "should" thought is unreasonable because she is late through no fault of her own. She is holding herself to a rigid set of rules even when it doesn't make sense.

What she does (or doesn't do) next as a result of her "I should" thought: She loses focus on the task at hand while in her mind she keeps criticizing herself for being late. As a result, she performs poorly at practice.

How she feels: She feels really down on herself and distracted and loses her drive to do her best.

How her body responds: Her muscles tense up, her jaw clenches, and she feels unable to run fast.

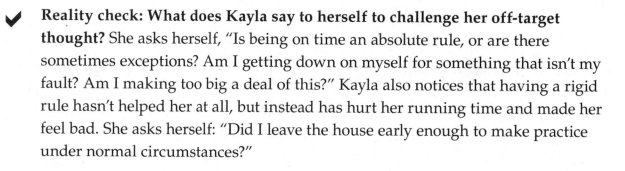

Reality check: What does Kayla say to herself to challenge her off-target thought? She asks herself, "Is being on time an absolute rule, or are there sometimes exceptions? Am I getting down on myself for something that isn't my fault? Am I making too big a deal of this?" Kayla also notices that having a rigid rule hasn't helped her at all, but instead has hurt her running time and made her feel bad. She asks herself: "Did I leave the house early enough to make practice under normal circumstances?"

Kayla's helpful thought and action plan: I'm almost never late. Today it couldn't be helped. I'll keep doing my best to be at practice before it starts. But I'll give myself a break when I don't have control. Even the coach ran late one time, and I didn't think less of him!

The payoff: How do the helpful thought and action plan improve Kayla's situation? By putting her lateness in perspective, Kayla is able to stop feeling so guilty and ashamed for being late. She feels relieved and optimistic that she'll be on time next week. Like Kayla, you'll soon see the power of thinking in terms of *I'd like to …* or *It would be nice if …* rather than *I should* or *I must!*

Activity 1: Practice the Steps

Jake has been looking forward for weeks to playing with his band in a battle of the bands competition to be held at his high school. But a snowstorm in a neighboring county prevents several of the bands from traveling, and the organizers decide to cancel the competition. They warn that it might be impossible to reschedule it. Jake gets so upset that he yells at his brother for playing his video games after school and decides not to bother doing any homework. He snaps at his mother when she asks what's wrong, telling her that the organizers are just being ridiculous. "So what if some bands can't come?" he says. "They should hold the competition anyway!"

What was Jake's off-target thinking error?

_____

_____

> What do you think Jake does (or doesn't do) next as a result of his "they should" thought?

_____

_____

♡ How do you think Jake feels? (Circle all that apply.)

Jealous	Panicked	Misunderstood	Angry
Inflexible	Sad	Disgusted	Annoyed
Confused	Alone	Worried	Helpless
Anxious	Intimidated	Stressed	Irritable
Distressed	Rejected	Hopeless	Energized
Gloomy	Hurt	Disappointed	Frustrated
Miserable	Neutral	Enraged	Satisfied

Other(s): _____

How do you think his body responds? (Circle all that apply.)

Feels shaky	Muscles tense	Gets warm	Heart pounds
Breathes fast	Feels sluggish	Gets sweaty	Feels dizzy
Stomach gets upset	Muscles relax	Frowns	Gets a headache
Face reddens	Gets fidgety	Feels heavy	Gets stiff
Neck stiffens	Feels tingly	Hands clench	Jaw tightens
Feels numb	Mouth gets dry	Feels spacey	Eyes roll

Other (s): _____

Reality check: What can Jake say to himself to challenge his off-target thought? When Jake looks at his "should" statement, he asks himself: "Is it reasonable for me to expect the competition organizers to do what I think they should do? What could they be thinking? Is my point of view reasonable or just my own preference?" Write down what Jake can say to himself after considering these questions to challenge his off-target thought.

_____

_____

_____

_____

Jake's helpful thought and action plan: I worked really hard getting ready for this competition. It would be nice if it could go on as planned, but the organizers have to worry about everybody's safety. I hope the competition can be rescheduled for later. But if not, we'll keep playing and see if we can find another event to perform at.

The payoff: How do the helpful thought and action plan improve Jake's situation? Consider the impact on his mood, physical sensations, behavior, and relationships.

_____

_____

_____

_____

Now that you've seen how turning a "should" into an "it would be nice if … " thought works, try taking these same steps yourself.

Activity 2: Change Your Own Thinking Habit

Remember a time when you set an unreasonable "should" rule for the way you, a friend, or your parent should act. Describe what happened and how your thinking was off-target.

_____

_____

_____

_____

> What did you do (or not do) next as a result of your "I should" or "he should" thought?

_____

_____

♡ How did this thought make you feel?

_____

_____

⩗ How did your body respond?

_____

_____

✔ Reality check: What could you have said to yourself to challenge your off-target thought? Some possibilities: "Were my expectations reasonable in this case? What if I substitute 'It would be nice if …' for the should statement? How did having a rigid rule help me? How did it hurt me?" After considering these questions, write down what you could have said to yourself to challenge the thought.

_____

_____

_____

_____

☁ What is a more realistic, helpful thought you might have had instead?

_____

_____

_____

_____

🚶 Describe your action plan:

_____

_____

_____

_____

🎖 The payoff: How would this helpful thought and action plan have improved your situation? Consider the impact on your mood, physical sensations, behavior, and relationships.

_____

_____

_____

By getting better at recognizing when your "shoulds" are actually your wishes, you will naturally become less demanding of others and more forgiving of yourself. The following exercise will give you more practice at seeing the difference.

Try It Out: *Should You?*

Read the following "should" statements and put a checkmark next to the ones you think are reasonable. Put an X next to the ones you think are not reasonable and might be better worded "It would be nice if ..." In the third column, briefly explain your answers.

Should Statements	√ or X	Explanation
I'm the fastest runner on the team. I should always win the hundred-yard dash.		
My sister was rude. She shouldn't be so disrespectful to my parents.		
The history test tomorrow is really important. I should study tonight.		
I've done most of the work on this group project. He should agree with my ideas!		
She's friends with my friends, so she should have invited me to the party, too.		
My parents really should come up with the money so I can go on the school ski trip.		
I should be able to stay up as late as I want.		
I don't care that my grandparents are visiting tonight. My parents should let me go out with my friends anyway.		
I get good grades, but I should always get A's.		
He shouldn't text while he's driving.		

Pausing to consider the rules you expect yourself and others to live by is important. It allows you to see which ones make sense and which ones are unrealistic and even harmful. Once you get the hang of doing that, you naturally become more flexible and resilient. That leaves you open to enjoying your life and other people as they are, instead of constantly feeling depressed, frustrated, or anxious about your rules not being met.

more for you to do

Learn a Bonus Skill: *Be Mindful of the Moment*

Mindfulness is a practice of being present in the moment. The goal is to let go of any thoughts of the past or future and become fully aware of the here and now—of what actually is. By practicing this skill of being completely in the moment, you develop the ability to experience what is happening without judging it, without imposing your ideas of the way things should be. At the same time, you free your mind of regrets about the past and of unnecessary worry about the future. Practicing mindfulness regularly can help you get unstuck when you find yourself thinking endlessly about unhappy events in the past. That type of ruminating contributes to sadness and depression. Becoming mindful can also cut short obsessive worrying about the future that can lead to anxiety.

Bringing your entire focus to the present moment can be difficult to do. It requires you to quiet the endless stream of thoughts flowing through your mind and just be! To become mindful, try sitting quietly with your eyes closed and pay attention only to your breathing, the feeling and the sound of air going in and out. Or listen with all of your attention to the sounds you hear. When your mind wanders, which is normal, simply focus again on your breathing or the sounds around you.

You don't have to sit still to be mindful. It's a good idea to practice being mindful in your activities throughout the day. Try focusing intently on each passing moment of your ride to school, for example, or keep your attention on each movement you make as you run or swim laps.

You can download "Be Mindful of the Moment," an audio meditation exercise, at http://www.newharbinger.com/38891.

Try It Out!

Find a wrapped piece of hard candy or a snack food—a bag of chips, for example. Focus all of your attention on it. Hold the item to your ear, and manipulate it gently with your fingers. Notice the sound. What do your fingers feel? Now open or remove the wrapping. What do you hear? How does the food feel in your hand? What does it look like? What range of colors does it have? Now take a sniff. Notice the blend of smells, without trying to think about what they are. Place the candy or a piece of the food on your tongue. Don't chew—just take a moment to detect the flavor and sensations as the candy melts or the chip softens. Tune in to the taste and the experience of slowly chewing and finally swallowing. When you eat mindfully, or do any activity mindfully, you begin to appreciate your moment-to-moment experience rather than getting stuck in the past or future.

Being mindful is a great way to interrupt problematic thinking. Rather than berating herself endlessly for being late for practice, for example, Kayla might have chosen to shift all of her attention to how the air and her body felt while she was running. Chances are that her performance would have been fine. And breaking that loop of "I should" thinking would have helped her put her lateness into perspective. Staying in the moment without judgment helps you dislodge the sad or anxious or angry thoughts that result from many of the off-target thinking patterns described in this book.

the big picture on "I should, you should" thinking

Adjusting your rigid "shoulds" so they become preferences and wishes will go a long way toward making you a more flexible, resilient person. Rather than automatically getting upset when a situation hasn't turned out the way you think it should have, you become able to consider whether what happened instead is actually okay or even great. You become less prone to depression about your imagined failings. And your friendships will flourish as you become less judgmental and more accepting. When you stop living by strict expectations, you might even find that you begin to enjoy the unexpected!

Remember:

- Teens who have the "I should, you should" habit hold themselves or others to a set of rigid and unreasonable rules. When their expectations are not met, they feel disappointed in themselves or frustrated and irritated at others.

- You can break this habit by taking a reality check. Ask yourself: "Is my should statement unreasonable? Is it really just what I would like to happen? How did having a rigid rule help me? How did it hurt?"

- Breaking this habit helps you become less hard on yourself and less critical of others. As you become more flexible, your self-image improves and you're less apt to withdraw from other people. Your relationships get better because you're easier to get along with.

chapter 6

The Fortune-Telling Habit

for you to know

If you have the fortune-telling habit, you jump to the conclusion in any given situation that you can predict the future—and that it's going to be unpleasant. *I'm going to fail geometry!* you might think, or *She'll say no if I ask her to hang out.* This thought habit has a lot in common with the catastrophizing habit (see chapter 2), which involves assuming that a catastrophe is about happen. Fortune-telling teens don't necessarily expect disaster, but they do think the future is going to be bleak. Unfortunately, by jumping to a conclusion that something disappointing is about to happen and getting stuck there, you leap right over what is actually true. And you completely ignore the various possibilities of what could come next. Since crystal balls rarely get it right, you often waste time getting upset or worrying for nothing!

Imagine that you hear an announcement when you're in the cafeteria at school calling you to the office. Someone with this habit might immediately think, *I'm in trouble!* In a case like this, the bad feeling that arises from fortune-telling would probably wear off quickly, as soon as you get the message that your mother will pick you up after school to go to the dentist. The problem gets a lot more serious, though, when you constantly predict that anything you try will end in failure or embarrassment. Teens who believe they're doomed to always mess up frequently either get discouraged and stop trying their hardest or feel so nervous when they have to perform that they freeze up. Then, guess what? The prophecy of failure is apt to come true. You give up and stop bothering to study when you predict that you'll fail geometry. You believe so strongly that you'll strike out when you're at bat that you're too distracted to focus on the ball. And then you start skipping practice and quit baseball.

The fortune-telling habit can be destructive to relationships, too. Suppose you see your boyfriend or girlfriend talking and laughing with someone he or she used to date. If you immediately predict that a breakup is in your future with no other reason to think so, then chances are you might get mad and do or say something impulsive that will only create conflict.

Assuming habitually that what will happen next is going to be bad news often leads to feelings of worry and discouragement. And the counterproductive behavior that often results, such as skipping baseball practice or giving up on geometry, can eventually lead to anxiety and depression.

The key to breaking this thinking habit is to pause and question your automatic predictions about the future. Ask yourself what evidence you have that a bad outcome is inevitable. Practice focusing on what is going on in the present and responding to it rather than jumping to conclusions about what will come next. Ask yourself how often your predictions have been wrong in the past. Remind yourself that you can be proactive. Are there actions you can take to affect the future you see?

The payoff of breaking this thinking habit is that you become more hopeful about the future. Taking a pause to evaluate a situation, rather than predicting an outcome, allows you to focus on and enjoy what is happening in the present. When you're optimistic, you're much more apt to try hard, persevere, and succeed. And you're much less likely to create conflict with your friends. Feelings of anxiety and depression lessen as your efforts show results.

for you to do

Your goal is to become an "I'll look before I leap" thinker. The cognitive restructuring exercises below will help you catch yourself when you jump to an unfavorable conclusion about the future. Can you find any evidence to support your fortune-telling thought? As you challenge your predictions about your own fate, you'll start to see helpful ways you can act in the here and now so the predictions don't turn into self-fulfilling prophecies. And as you stop yourself from predicting what awful thing a friend or family member is about to do, your interactions with other people will get more satisfying.

Try It Out: *Cognitive Restructuring*

Since getting his learner's permit, Charlie has practiced for weeks to take his driver's test. He's been feeling pretty excited about having his license because he wants to be able to drive to games and other school events like his brother does. But he blows the parking part of the test and ends up failing. Rather than looking at what he did wrong and thinking about what he can do to improve his chances of passing next time, he thinks, *I'm such a bad driver. I won't even get my license before graduation!* He feels really hopeless as he imagines next year without being able to drive.

💭 **Charlie's off-target thinking error:** Without any evidence about what will happen in the future, Charlie makes a negative prediction that he won't be driving at all next year. He doesn't take into account that he can be proactive. He has some control over how much effort he puts into practicing.

❯ **What he does (or doesn't do) next as a result of his fortune-telling thought:** He lets his dad drive home from the test site and tells him, "Practicing more is pointless! I give up!"

♡ **How he feels:** He feels discouraged about his chances of ever passing the driver's test.

🏃 **How his body responds:** He becomes listless, his shoulders droop, and he lacks energy.

✔ **Reality check: What does Charlie say to himself to challenge his off-target thought?** He checks to see if there's any evidence that he can't get his license before graduation. He asks himself, "How do I know for sure I can't pass next time? What power do I have to predict the future?" He remembers that other friends have failed and taken the test again successfully within a few weeks. One friend even failed the test twice before passing on the third try.

🏃 **Charlie's helpful thought and action plan:** Just because I didn't pass once doesn't mean I won't next time. I'll practice for the next few weeks, especially the maneuvers that are hard for me. And I'll pick a test date for some time next month.

🎖 **The payoff: How do the helpful thought and action plan improve Charlie's situation?** By realizing that he can't know for sure what will happen in the future—and that he actually has a lot of power to affect what happens—he becomes energized. He feels more hopeful and motivated to work hard on his driving. As you gain experience stopping yourself from jumping to negative conclusions about the future, you, like Charlie, will feel more powerful to affect events.

Activity 1: Practice the Steps

Sophia's dad has been transferred to a new city, and it means she has to switch schools in the middle of tenth grade. As soon as she hears the news, she jumps to the conclusion that, because she tends to be so quiet, she won't fit in. Nobody will notice her or like her, she predicts. And besides, she thinks, by tenth grade, everybody will already have enough friends! Without friends, she'll feel awkward all the time, and high school will be no fun.

💭 What was Sophia's off-target thinking error?

_____

_____

❭ What do you think Sophia does (or doesn't do) next as a result of her fortune-telling thought?

_____

_____

♡ How do you think Sophia feels? (Circle all that apply.)

Vulnerable	Disgusted	Calm	Lonely
Confused	Annoyed	Grateful	Angry
Embarrassed	Worried	Helpless	Anxious
Intimidated	Distressed	Uncomfortable	Mad
Fearful	Stressed	Irritable	Rejected
Tearful	Discouraged	Panicked	Lost
Self-conscious	Miserable	Envious	Misunderstood

Other(s): _____

How do you think her body responds? (Circle all that apply.)

Feels shaky	Muscles tense	Heart races	Gets lump in throat
Breathes fast	Feels sluggish	Gets sweaty	Feels cold
Stomach gets upset	Muscles relax	Frowns	Gets a headache
Feels energetic	Face reddens	Gets fidgety	Heart pounds
Hands clench	Jaw tightens	Toes clench	Gets breathless
Feels clammy	Feels cold	Feels light-headed	Feels nauseous

Other(s): _____

✔ Reality check: What can Sophia say to herself to challenge her off-target thought? She stops for a moment and thinks about whether she has any evidence that she'll have a terrible time at her new school. She reminds herself that she fits in fine at her current school. She asks herself, "Since I've never even visited the school, how do I know what it's like? How do I know the kids there won't be friendly?" Write down what Sophia can say to herself after considering these questions to challenge her off-target thought.

_____

_____

_____

_____

Sophia's helpful thought and action plan: I may be quiet, but I have plenty of friends here, and I have no reason to believe that I won't fit in at my new school. It's normal to be a little nervous at first in a new place, but this move also can be exciting. I'll see if I can meet some kids in the neighborhood, and I'll check the website to see what activities I could join. I'll be as friendly as I can be. I'll make the best of it!

The payoff: How do the helpful thought and action plan improve Sophia's situation? Consider the impact on her mood, physical sensations, behavior, and relationships.

_____

_____

_____

_____

You, too, can put your negative crystal ball away and take realistic stock of the present! Try taking these steps yourself.

Activity 2: Change Your Own Thinking Habit

Remember a time when you used your crystal ball to predict that something bad would happen when there was no good reason to think so. Describe what happened and how your thoughts were off-target.

_____

_____

_____

_____

> What did you do (or not do) next as a result of your fortune-telling thought?

_____

_____

_____

_____

♡ How did this thought make you feel?

_____

_____

 How did your body respond?

_____

_____

✔ Reality check: What could you have said to yourself to challenge your off-target thought? Some possibilities: "Is my prediction reasonable in this case? What evidence do I have to base my fortune-telling on? How often am I right when I jump to the conclusion that something bad will happen?" After considering these questions, write down what you could have said to yourself to challenge the thought.

_____

_____

_____

_____

☁ What is a more realistic, helpful thought you might have had instead?

_____

_____

_____

_____

🏃 Describe your action plan:

_____

_____

_____

_____

🎖 The payoff: How would this helpful thought and action plan have improved your situation? Consider the impact on your mood, physical sensations, behavior, and relationships.

_____

_____

_____

_____

When you stop jumping to the conclusion that something negative is going to happen, you become calmer. You're more able to see what is occurring now and what opportunities lie ahead. And when you're more hopeful that something good could happen, you're more motivated to try to make that come true.

Try It Out: *What's the Evidence?*

Let's get some practice looking for evidence. Think about where you go for evidence when you're working on a school project, for example. You can gather facts by doing research online or in the library or by asking other people for information. Another good source of evidence is past behavior or experiences.

Read the predictions below, and in the space underneath each one, list two types of evidence you could find that would either support or refute the prediction. You may be surprised to find that the evidence helps increase the odds of a positive outcome instead!

Example: *Taking this road trip with my parents is going to be so boring!*

Evidence:

1. *previous road trips with parents*

2. *research on what you can do for fun during a long car ride, as well as interesting activities at all the stops along the way*

I'm going to have an anxiety attack at the party!

Evidence:

1. _____

2. _____

There's no way our group project will get done on time!

Evidence:

1. _____

2. _____

My cousin won't want to hang out with me when his family comes for winter break.

Evidence:

1. _____

2. _____

Our basketball team is sure to lose the big game this weekend.

Evidence:

1. _____

2. _____

Our day trip to the beach tomorrow is going to get rained out!

Evidence:

1. _____

2. _____

the big picture on fortune-telling

The habit of making negative predictions about the future can damage your performance and your self-confidence and interfere with your friendships. When you constantly doubt your own abilities, you may lose hope and stop trying. And jumping to the conclusion that someone else is going to disappoint you is bound to affect how you interact with that person. By paying close attention to the present and becoming an "I'll look before I leap!" thinker instead, you begin to see—and believe—that many possibilities exist. Believing that you have the power to affect which one comes true makes you a more resilient person.

Remember:

- Teens with the fortune-telling habit jump to the conclusion that they're bound to mess up or that a future event will be a disappointment. They either get really down on themselves and feel unmotivated and depressed, or they feel resentful.

- You can train yourself to stop fortune-telling by taking a reality check. Ask yourself: "Do I have enough evidence to draw conclusions about what will happen? What makes me so sure that a bad outcome is inevitable? Do I have any power to affect what comes next?"

- Stopping yourself from leaping to negative conclusions will help you become more hopeful and optimistic. You'll begin to see the future as filled with opportunities and will feel much more confident about taking advantage of them!

chapter 7

The Mind-Reading Habit

for you to know

The mind-reading habit is a very common type of thinking error that involves jumping to conclusions without any reason. When you make the mistake of mind-reading, you automatically assume you know what someone else is thinking. And you're sure that it's something hostile or unflattering about you. You're convinced you're right about what's going on in the other person's head without the slightest bit of evidence. Usually you do this without even realizing that there could be other more logical conclusions to consider. In fact, the chances are good that the other person isn't even thinking about you at all!

Imagine, for example, that you're at a party and the girl you're talking to says, "I'm going to grab a soda," and walks away. What's your immediate reaction? If you have the mind-reading habit, rather than taking her word for it that she's thirsty, you might say to yourself, "She thinks I'm boring!" As a result, you might start worrying so much about being boring that it interferes with all of your other conversations. Or you might just walk away from the party and miss out on the fun. It's also possible that you might get super annoyed and blurt out something sarcastic, causing a tense interaction when your thought isn't justified.

Or suppose you overhear your mother making a big deal to your grandparents about the A your brother got on his algebra final. Since she doesn't mention you at all, you think, *I guess Mom must really be disappointed in my grades.*

Not surprisingly, this type of negative thinking can make you feel really down on yourself. It can also make you feel insecure and awkward in social situations. Teens who worry that other people are judging them critically are likely to start dreading such interactions and avoiding other people. Or they start feeling mad about imagined slights. Over time, mind-readers become more prone to experiencing social anxiety, self-doubt, or anger. When you doubt yourself, it's very common to be fearful about stretching yourself—to meet new people, to apply for a job, to try out for a team. When anxiety causes you to isolate yourself from other people, your friendships will suffer. And when you misinterpret what other people's actions mean, it's very common to respond in a hurt or hostile way that harms your relationships.

The key to breaking this thinking habit is to recognize what you're doing each time you begin to mind-read. Pause to remind yourself that nobody can read minds. Then, really look at and listen to the other person. What facial expressions, body language, and words are you seeing and hearing? As you try and interpret the situation, look for all the more positive and likely possibilities. Sometimes, of course, you'll examine the evidence and know that you messed up, and that your friends or parents are frowning at you with good reason. When you read the situation accurately, though, you can take action and handle it.

One of the best effects of breaking this habit is that, when you stop assuming people are thinking badly of you, you become more comfortable and self-confident in social situations. You get braver about taking chances. Rather than avoiding other people, you'll feel good about spending time with friends and might even be the one to reach out to make plans! Feelings of social anxiety or anger that arise from reading other people's thoughts melt away when you gather the facts and do a better job of gauging what's really happening.

for you to do

Your goal is to become a "What else could he mean?" thinker. Using the steps of cognitive restructuring, you'll get the hang of stopping yourself from jumping to conclusions about what other people are thinking. The idea is to try to see what is actually going on rather than automatically assuming that other people are evaluating you and making negative judgments. You'll practice challenging faulty conclusions by coming up with other possible interpretations of the person's expressions, gestures or actions.

Try It Out: *Cognitive Restructuring*

When Nick is getting his lunch, he notices a group of his science classmates eating together at a nearby table. He spots an empty seat at the table and starts to walk toward the group. One of the girls says something that causes a big laugh as they glance in his direction. Nick stops short and tenses up, thinking, *They're laughing at me!* He is embarrassed, feels dejected, and heads for another table.

☁ **Nick's off-target thinking error:** He is absolutely sure that his classmates are making fun of him. He's convinced he is right even in the absence of any evidence that the laughter had anything to do with him.

❯ **What he does (or doesn't do) next as a result of his mind-reading thought:** He sits by himself and avoids his classmates.

♡ **How he feels:** He feels anxious and humiliated.

👤 **How his body responds:** His stomach tightens and his face feels hot.

✔ **Reality check: What does Nick say to himself to challenge his off-target thought?** Nick examines the evidence that the group is laughing at him. He acknowledges that it's a possibility, but can see many more likely explanations for the laughter when he challenges his thought. He says to himself: "How do I know for certain what they're thinking, or even that they're thinking about me? What else could they be laughing about? They could be talking about school or a funny video. They've never made fun of me or given me a hard time before. What makes me think they are laughing at me?"

Nick's helpful thought and action plan: It looks like they're having a good time. Since they haven't ever put me down before, they probably aren't now. This probably doesn't even have anything to do with me. Next time something like this happens, I'll take a chance and sit with them—and find out what's so funny.

The payoff: How the helpful thought and action plan improve Nick's situation: By recognizing that he has imagined a situation that is probably not true, he becomes more confident that he's perfectly likable and would be welcome in the group. Rather than avoiding people, he also feels much more open to reaching out and being friendly with others at school. With practice, you, like Nick, can get better at catching yourself in the habit of mind-reading earlier and earlier. Ideally, you can recognize your thinking error in time to do a quick reality check before you start feeling gloomy, withdraw, and miss out on fun with your friends!

Activity 1: Practice the Steps

One day Emily is studying in the media center. She overhears her good friend Madison ask another friend to go to the movies on Saturday and get pizza afterward. Since Madison doesn't include her, Emily thinks, *Madison must not want to be my friend anymore.*

What was Emily's off-target thinking error?

_____

_____

> What do you think she does (or doesn't do) next as a result of her mind-reading thought?

_____

_____

♡ How do you think Emily feels? (Circle all that apply.)

Sad	Confused	Annoyed	Angry
Lonely	Worried	Helpless	Anxious
Intimidated	Fearful	Stressed	Irritable
Distressed	Uncomfortable	Agitated	Gloomy
Tearful	Shaky	Panicked	Rejected
Disappointed	Mad	Vulnerable	Hurt
Frustrated	Miserable	Envious	Hopeless

Other(s): _____

How do you think her body responds? (Circle all that apply.)

Feels sluggish	Fists clench	Muscles feel tense	Feels dizzy
Gets shaky	Heart races	Feels tingly	Breathes rapidly
Gets sweaty	Feels heavy	Gets lump in throat	Muscles relax
Hands get clammy	Stomach churns	Face reddens	Gets fidgety
Face scrunches up	Neck tightens	Chest tightens	Stomach gets upset
Feels warm	Shoulders hunch	Feels chills	Frowns

Other(s): _____

Reality check: What can Emily say to herself to challenge her off-target thought? When Emily weighs the evidence that Madison doesn't like her as much as she thought, she asks herself: "How do I know for certain what she is thinking? What are some more likely interpretations of the situation? Do I always include Madison when I make a plan? What would I say to a friend who does this kind of mind-reading?" Write down what Emily can say to herself after considering these questions to challenge her off-target thought.

_____

_____

_____

_____

Emily's helpful thought and action plan: Madison and I both have other friends, and it's fine to get together with different people at different times. I'll call Jessica and see if she can get together on Saturday. I'll plan something with Madison for another time.

The payoff: How do the helpful thought and action plan improve Emily's situation? Consider the impact on her mood, physical sensations, behavior, and relationships.

_____

_____

_____

_____

Now that you've helped Emily break her mind-reading habit, take these thought-correcting steps yourself.

Activity 2: Change Your Own Thinking Habit

Think of a time when you engaged in mind-reading, interpreting someone's actions to mean he or she was judging you negatively or putting you down. Describe what happened and how your thoughts were off-target.

_____

_____

_____

_____

> What did you do (or not do) next as a result of your mind-reading thought?

_____

_____

_____

_____

♡ How did this thought make you feel?

_____

_____

♦ How did your body respond?

_____

_____

✔ Reality check: What could you have said to yourself to challenge your off-target thought? Some possibilities: "How do I know for sure what he or she is thinking? How do I know it's about me?" Notice what supports your assumption and what argues against it. For example: "What are some more likely interpretations of the situation? What would I tell a friend who is mind-reading like I just did?" After considering these questions, write down what you could have said to yourself to challenge the thought.

_____

_____

_____

_____

☁ What is a more helpful, realistic thought you might have had instead?

_____

_____

_____

_____

🏃 Describe your action plan:

_____

_____

_____

_____

🎖 The payoff: How would this helpful thought and action plan have improved your situation? Consider the impact on your mood, physical sensations, behavior, and relationships.

_____

_____

_____

_____

Taking these steps to catch and challenge your mind-reading thoughts will help you learn to react to what is real rather than to what you imagine is true. And you'll soon discover that most of the time what you've imagined is far worse than reality!

Try It Out: *Write a Story*

Write a short story about a girl who breaks up with the classmate she's been dating for three months. The problem that causes their split is that she has been doing some mind-reading. Describe her mind-reading error and include what happens when she realizes her mistake. How does that help her?

As you can see, jumping to the conclusion that someone else is thinking critically about you can have a very bad effect on your relationships. Think about it: Can you ever really be sure what someone else is thinking unless he or she tells you? In general, pausing to weigh the evidence of what is really going on in your interactions with friends and family members is necessary to form and sustain healthy relationships.

more for you to do

Learn a Bonus Skill: *Show Yourself Compassion*

Whenever you find yourself believing that there's something wrong with you, or that someone else thinks badly of you, it can help a lot to treat yourself with compassion. It's human nature to offer kindness and forgiveness to other people when they make mistakes or do something silly or even hurtful because everyone understands that no one is perfect. Yet it's often really tough to be similarly kind to yourself. Practicing the skill of showing yourself compassion helps you silence the harsh self-talk running on an endless loop in your mind. That nagging voice in your head—everyone has one—is usually busy harping on all of your supposed failings. But it can be trained to pat you on the back instead. The idea isn't to make excuses for your mistakes. Instead, you put them in perspective by giving yourself credit for all your good points, too.

Start by reflecting on your best qualities and achievements and also think back on recent slip-ups you've made that have bothered you. Then spend a minute appreciating all of the wonderful things about you and accept that you're going to make mistakes because you're human. You might say to yourself, "I have many great qualities, and I have family and friends who care about me." Practice being forgiving: "I can't believe I said that, but everybody says dumb things sometimes." As you get better at giving yourself credit, you'll become more conscious of your many strengths. And you'll be less likely to jump to the conclusion that other people are judging you harshly.

Try It Out!

Write down an example of the negative self-talk you hear most frequently from your inner critic (for example, "That was such a stupid thing to do!" or "They must think I'm a real loser!").

_____

_____

Next, list five of your strengths. (Use the examples below to get you started thinking.) Write a kind, compassionate statement, one for each of these five strengths, that your inner voice can say instead (for example, "Even though I didn't do well on the math quiz, I am hard-working and a good student.").

Good listener	Thoughtful	Caring
Outgoing	Creative	Hard-working
Good friend	Organized	Good student

Strength	Compassionate Statement

The advantage to practicing self-compassion is that it reminds you that you have a lot to offer. When you feel good about yourself, you're less likely to assume that people are critical of you. You're also less likely to feel anxious or to have big ups and downs in your moods. Giving yourself a break when you make mistakes, and believing that you're a worthy and capable person anyway, gives you the confidence to persevere when the going gets tough.

the big picture on mind-reading

Teens who mind-read are often completely wrong in their conclusions. As a result, they feel down or socially anxious, and often withdraw into themselves. When you pause and look for all of the more likely interpretations of a situation, chances are you'll find a number of possibilities that are not disapproving judgments of you. That more realistic outlook allows you to feel less anxious—and, as a result, you're open to new experiences and more apt to have fun!

Remember:

- Teens with the mind-reading habit jump to the conclusion that someone else is thinking about them and that the thought is critical.

- You can break this habit by taking a reality check. Ask yourself: "How do I know for sure what he or she is thinking? What are more likely interpretations?"

- When you take this more realistic view, you are less likely to feel socially anxious and limit your activities with other people. Rather than withdrawing, you have the confidence to stretch and try new things.

chapter 8

The Blaming Habit

for you to know

You probably have figured out by now that the day-to-day events of your life rarely go just the way you'd like them to. So every day, you're called on to be flexible when you or your friends or family members make moves you don't like or when stuff just happens. An ability to go with the flow and change course as needed is key to finding pleasure in your activities rather than being constantly disappointed. But many teens have the "blaming" habit and get stuck immediately on the angry or guilty thought, *It's all your fault!* or *It's all my fault!* Anytime something goes wrong, some teens place the blame for their misery on somebody else. Other teens tend to beat themselves up, taking on all the blame. So they either feel enraged and victimized, or they feel guilt and shame. Does that sound familiar?

Suppose your friend Sarah comes home with you after school, not bothering to call her dad to let him know where she is. He phones her and is angry that she's broken the rules again. Now she's grounded and can't go with you to a concert. If you have the tendency to immediately blame others, you might think, *Sarah's father spoiled all my fun!* You feel so bitter and angry at him that you mope around and can't even think about trying to find someone else to go with you. When you rush to blame somebody else for every disappointment, even when there's a good reason for the disappointment, you spend a lot of time and energy being angry and resentful. You also don't own up to any responsibility you share in the outcome.

Or suppose you get stuck in heavy traffic driving your friends to the movies. As a result, you miss the first few minutes and everybody has to go without popcorn. You think, *It's all my fault that we were late!* You feel so guilty and worried about whether your friends are disappointed that you can't concentrate on the movie. Always taking all the blame can make you feel so down on yourself that you withdraw and don't bother trying to fix the problem. Eventually, this gloom and passivity can lead to depression, anxiety, and low self-esteem.

It's appropriate to expect an apology from someone who truly causes you harm. It's also important, of course, to take responsibility for your actions when you've made a bad decision or hurt somebody. But immediately jumping to place blame (or take it on) rarely, if ever, makes the situation better. Often, you are not even seeing clearly what actually happened. Maybe no one is at fault! Or maybe a number of factors together have pitched you this curve ball. What you really need to do (rather than placing blame) is to think about other ways of looking at the situation, find a creative solution, and take action.

The key to breaking this thinking habit is to recognize that everybody goofs up, and in many cases, the circumstances are beyond anyone's control. Rushing to blame someone else or yourself for a disappointment or bad result rarely does any good. It's possible that you might need to first accept responsibility for whatever part you play, and apologize if appropriate. That's a healthy response. But rather than getting stuck on fault and blame, the idea is to ask, "What can I do now to make the best of this situation?"

The payoff to taking blame out of the equation is that you begin reacting in a more creative, upbeat way when things don't work out the way you expected them to. You start to see that you have the power to find fixes or to take different paths. That flexible, can-try attitude will help you feel good about your abilities. And becoming more accepting of other people's actions will go a long way toward improving your relationships.

for you to do

Your goal is to become a "This is a bummer. How can I respond to this?" thinker. You'll get the hang of pausing whenever you catch yourself thinking, *It's all my fault!* or *It's all his fault!* to take a realistic look at what has happened. Maybe no one is at fault. Or perhaps there are a number of factors that share responsibility. The exercises that follow will teach you to quickly move beyond the question of blame to brainstorming positive steps you can take next.

Try It Out: *Cognitive Restructuring*

Damon and his teammates were sure they had a good shot at winning the football game against their number one rival, the Bulldogs. They played really hard and were a touchdown ahead at halftime. But with three minutes to go, they lost the ball when the quarterback threw a pass that went a little wide, and Damon couldn't get to it. The ball was intercepted, and the game ended in a loss. Damon spent the whole bus ride home berating himself for not running faster. It was all his fault, he thought, that the team had lost.

Damon's off-target thinking error: Damon's automatic thought is that he wasn't quite good enough, and therefore all of the blame for losing the game is his. While it's important to always try one's best, he is ignoring the fact that the whole team contributed to the results, and that other teams sometimes have a better game.

What he does (or doesn't do) next as a result of his "It's all my fault!" thought: He slumps down in his seat. He replays missing the pass over and over in his mind, blaming himself. And he avoids talking with anyone else.

How he feels: He feels down and disgusted with himself. He feels alone and worried that he has disappointed everyone on the team.

How his body responds: His hands feel clammy, and he feels nauseous. At the same time, he feels sluggish, as if he has zero energy.

✔ **Reality check: What does Damon say to himself to challenge his off-target thought?** Damon looks at what went right in the game as well as what went wrong. He thinks about the effort he and his team put forth. He tells himself, "That was a tough pass, and I ran my fastest." He asks, "Am I being fair to myself to take on all the responsibility for whether the team loses or wins? Am I blaming myself for something that isn't my fault?"

🏃 **Damon's helpful thought and action plan:** I did my best, and so did my team. We can't win all the games. Maybe the Bulldogs played better than we did. That doesn't make losing my fault. I am going to focus on what I did well and keep practicing. And I'll compliment the other guys on their plays.

🎖 **The payoff: How do the helpful thought and action plan improve Damon's situation?** As soon as Damon puts the game in perspective, he feels a sense of relief and a surge of energy. He relaxes and smiles, and joins in the fun on the bus. When he acts friendly, his teammates respond to him in a positive way. Like Damon, you can stop yourself from thinking *It's all my fault!* and take a more realistic view of the situation. When you do, you'll begin to feel more confident rather than down on yourself—and more optimistic.

Activity 1: Practice the Steps

Annika is really annoyed when she gets back her English paper on *The Call of the Wild* and sees that her teacher, Mr. Henson, gave her a C. The problem was that she hadn't given enough biographical information about the author, Jack London. Even though she can see that the kid sitting next to her got an A, she blames Mr. Henson for her poor grade. "He's a terrible teacher!" she tells herself. "He gave us really bad instructions! This is all his fault!" By dismissing Mr. Henson's feedback on her essay and blaming him for her grade, she doesn't think about whether she can take any steps to help herself. She closes her mind to ideas about what she could do to improve her work in the future.

💭 What was Annika's off-target thinking error?

_____

_____

> What do you think she does (or doesn't do) next as a result of her "It's all his fault!" thought?

_____

_____

♡ How do you think Annika feels? (Circle all that apply.)

Disgusted	Annoyed	Angry	Sad
Furious	Worried	Helpless	Anxious
Intimidated	Fearful	Stressed	Irritable
Distressed	Uncomfortable	Worthless	Gloomy
Tearful	Shaky	Panicked	Scared
Lost	Rejected	Disappointed	Frustrated
Hurt	Enraged	Furious	Confused

Other(s): _____

How do you think her body responds? (Circle all that apply.)

Gets shaky	Muscles feel tense	Heart races	Gets lump in throat
Breathes rapidly	Feels sluggish	Gets sweaty	Feels cold
Stomach gets upset	Muscles relax	Frowns	Gets headache
Eyes roll	Gets fidgety	Face scrunches up	Fists clench
Jaw clenches	Shoulders slump	Mouth gets dry	Hands get clammy
Feels hot	Feels numb	Feels tingly	Stomach flutters

Other(s): _____

Reality check: What can Annika say to herself to challenge her off-target thought? Knowing that she wants to get better grades, Annika can start by taking an honest look at Mr. Henson's comments. She asks herself, "Do his comments make sense? Did the other students understand what he expected?" She examines the evidence that her teacher grades unfairly and asks herself, "What could I have done differently to get a better grade?" Write down what Annika can say to herself after considering these questions to challenge her off-target thought.

_____

_____

_____

_____

Annika's helpful thought and action plan: When something goes wrong, it's usually not just one person's fault. I worked really hard on this paper, but I did miss the fact that I needed more biographical information. I'll pay closer attention to the directions next time.

The payoff: How do the helpful thought and action plan improve Annika's situation? Consider the impact on her mood, physical sensations, behavior, and relationships.

_____

_____

_____

_____

Now that you've seen how the off-target blaming habit can be harmful and how this thinking error can be tackled, try taking these steps yourself.

Activity 2: Change Your Own Thinking Habit

Remember a time when you unreasonably blamed yourself or someone else for a disappointment. Describe what happened and how your thinking was off-target.

_____

_____

_____

_____

> **What did you do (or not do) next as a result of your blaming thought?**

_____

_____

_____

_____

♡ **How did this thought make you feel?**

_____

_____

♦ **How did your body respond?**

_____

_____

_____

_____

✔ Reality check: What could you have said to yourself to challenge your off-target thought? Some possibilities: "Am I being fair to myself by taking all the blame? Or am I being fair to others by blaming them? How does blaming myself or someone else help me? What are all the factors that may have contributed to this situation? Were some or all of these factors beyond anyone's control?" After considering these questions, write down what you could have said to yourself to challenge the thought.

_____

_____

_____

💭 What is a more realistic, helpful thought you might have had instead?

_____

_____

_____

_____

🏃 Describe your action plan:

_____

_____

_____

_____

🎖 The payoff: How would this helpful thought and action plan have improved your situation? Consider the impact on your mood, physical sensations, behavior, and relationships.

_____

_____

_____

_____

With practice, you'll get better at noticing yourself immediately assigning blame. A quick reality check will help you take a more balanced view of your situation. You'll start focusing instead on what to do next. You'll discover that it feels good when every disappointment doesn't lead to automatic feelings of guilt and shame or anger and resentment. Instead, you'll start to be flexible and creative about those next steps!

Try It Out: *Slice the Pie*

Think of another time when you were really upset and blamed yourself or someone else for an outcome you didn't like. You or another person may have been partly responsible. After you pause for a reality check, make a list of all the factors that contributed to the outcome in the spaces below. For example: "It was pouring, so traffic was really slow." Or, "The test covered material that we didn't review in class." Or, "The plans changed because my brother got sick."

Situation: _____

Factors that contributed to the outcome:

1. _____

2. _____

3. _____

4. _____

5. _____

6. _____

Now, create a pie chart using the circle below that shows a realistic breakdown of how much each of these various factors contributed to that outcome.

Some bad outcomes are clearly your fault. When you fail a test because you just didn't bother studying, most or all of the responsibility probably lies with you. And sometimes other people bear responsibility for your hurt—for example, when your boyfriend or girlfriend goes out with someone else behind your back. But usually when teens who have the blaming habit fill in their pie chart realistically, they can see that multiple factors contribute to most disappointments. And lots of times— when the weather or heavy traffic is the problem like—an outcome can't be helped and blame is simply beside the point.

more for you to do

Learn a Bonus Skill: *Change Your Point of View*

The blaming habit and other forms of off-target thinking involve having a very narrow (and faulty) perspective on the world around you. Your mind gets stuck on what you think is the true picture (*I'm so slow and clumsy!* or *He's a bad coach!*) when what you really need to do is step back and take in the bigger picture (*We made a few mistakes, but the other team played better and is undefeated!*).

It can help a lot to practice the skill of changing your point of view. That means deliberately looking around and making note of the parts of the whole picture that you've missed. To get the idea, take a look at the photos of the carpet below. Notice how the pattern looks entirely different when you step back and broaden your focus.

Try It Out!

Now close your eyes and imagine that you're in a baseball stadium, walking the diamond from home plate to first, second, and third base, and back home again. How does your perspective of the stadium and the field change as you move around the bases?

When you pause to change your point of view, you begin to understand that the truth is often quite different than your narrow view leads you to believe. You gain an understanding of where other people are coming from. The power of being able to appreciate other people's reasoning, hopes, and needs is that it makes you an empathetic person. Feeling empathy for others is key to happy relationships. And seeing your own goofs with this greater understanding lets you feel less critical of yourself.

the big picture on blaming

The automatic habit of blaming yourself or other people when something unwelcome happens often gives you a highly distorted view of reality. And it doesn't do you any good, because blaming doesn't fix anything. It just leaves you feeling all roiled up with guilt or anger. When the blaming impulse strikes, it's much healthier to figure out whether anyone is actually at fault and what all the many contributing factors are. When you step back and see the whole picture, you're much better able to adjust your expectations and take action with flexibility and good humor.

Remember:

- Teens with the blaming habit either think *It's all my fault!* and feel guilty or *It's all his fault!* and feel anger and resentment.

- You can break this habit by taking a reality check. Ask yourself: "Is anyone responsible? What are all the contributing causes?"

- When you take this more realistic view, your feelings of guilt or anger vanish. Rather than getting stuck on who's at fault, you can generate lots of ideas about what to do next and take action.

chapter 9

The "It's Not Fair!" Habit

for you to know

The "It's not fair!" habit is one of the most common thinking errors. When you have this habit, your beliefs about what ought to happen in your life are based on the unrealistic expectation that the world always works according to strict standards of justice and equal treatment—and that you know exactly what those standards are. *It's not fair that I have to study for my test while my brother goes to the movies!* you might think. Or *It's not fair that we can't get a dog when all my friends have dogs!* Rather than understanding that life is a complicated and often chaotic journey that's different for everybody and not always fair, you seem to expect that someone should be keeping score to make sure you don't get shortchanged. When you think this way, it's impossible to take other people's reasons and desires into account or to be glad for them when they get opportunities that you don't.

For example, teens often expect that they should have all the same privileges their friends enjoy. So when you and your best friend get different curfews, or he gets to take over his grandparents' old car while you're dependent on getting rides everywhere, you're going to feel badly mistreated if you have this habit. "It's not fair that I have to be home by 10:00 p.m. when Terry can stay out until 11:00!" you yell at your parents. Or "I can't believe that you won't let me have a car, too!"

Obviously, there are times when justice is important and worth standing up for. But demanding that your personal standards of fair play must always be met leaves you feeling constantly like a helpless victim and disappointed or angry when reality doesn't cooperate. This kind of off-target thinking can be very hard on your friendships because you're often tense and grouchy when you feel unfairly treated. Your relationship with your parents will suffer, too, if you're often angry about the decisions they make. And feeling like a victim when obstacles arise in your path can cause you to mope around and become depressed rather than learning to problem solve. You miss the chance to be proactive and make the most of your situation—skills that make you more resilient and better able to bounce back from disappointments!

The key to breaking the "It's not fair!" habit is to remind yourself (until you accept it) that achieving equality in all circumstances is an impossibility. All sorts of joys and surprises and disappointments are in store for you, and you'll handle the letdowns much better if you can accept what comes and roll with it rather than getting stuck in bitterness. Often, there are good reasons for the decisions your parents or teachers or friends make that you think are unfair. Trying to imagine what those reasons are can remind you that other people's needs and wishes matter, too. In fact, part of the work of adolescence is to learn how to make changes when life doesn't go your way, to cooperate with people, and to negotiate. As you practice taking a reality check, you'll get better at distinguishing between off-target "It's not fair!" thinking and cases of true injustice that may deserve some attention.

The payoff of breaking the "It's not fair!" habit is that your anger dissolves as you grow more accepting of the way things are. As you begin to look at and appreciate other people's points of view, you can start to come up with positive steps to take rather than seeing yourself as a victim. You might ask your parents to consider a later curfew if you make it home by 10:00 p.m. for the next six months, say. And you might decide that if you can't have a dog, it would be fun to start a dog-walking business. Responding to disappointments creatively rather than angrily feels good. You'll be a happier person and a better friend.

for you to do

Your goal is to become an "It is what it is" thinker. By catching yourself in "It's not fair!" statements and examining whether or not they're realistic, you'll let go of the notion that you're somehow owed equal treatment. You'll begin to see that other people have reasons for the decisions they make and that it's more helpful to stop thinking in terms of fairness. Your aim is to take what comes calmly and with an open mind, and problem solve so you can respond to it in a positive way.

Try It Out: *Cognitive Restructuring*

How to break the "It's Not Fair!" habit: Emma has been looking forward all week to going indoor rock climbing with her friend Karima on Friday after school. But just before they leave, Emma gets a text from her mother saying that something has come up at work and she has to stay late to meet a deadline. Emma needs to get home to fix her younger brother dinner and stay with him for the evening. *No!* Emma thinks. *That's not fair!* Because she gets stuck on that thought, she feels miserable for the rest of the evening.

Emma's off-target thinking error: She immediately and automatically assumes that what she wants is the right and fair outcome. Emma can't look beyond her disappointment and feelings of injustice to appreciate that her mother and her family also have legitimate needs.

What she does (or doesn't do) next as a result of her "It's not fair!" thought: She texts her mother back rudely, accusing her of being unfair. She comes home, but spends the evening sulking and yells at her brother for no reason.

How she feels: She feels furious at first, and is resentful and irritable throughout the evening.

How her body responds: She clenches her hands, and her stomach churns. She tenses up with anger.

✔ **Reality check: What does Emma say to herself to challenge her off-target thought?** Emma considers whether it's realistic to believe that life is always fair. She also thinks about whether it makes sense that her wishes always matter more than anyone else's. She asks herself, "Could Mom help it that she needed to stay at work? Did she change the plans just to be mean to me? I can arrange to go rock climbing another time."

Emma's helpful thought and action plan: I'm bummed that I have to miss out on rock climbing tonight, but I can see my mother's point of view. I'll apologize to her for being rude. I'll have other opportunities to do something fun with Karima.

The payoff: How do the helpful thought and action plan improve Emma's situation? By acknowledging her family's needs, Emma lets her frustration and anger go. Being willing to go with the flow improves her interactions with her mother and brother and puts her in a better mood. She feels less agitated and stressed out, and her body calms. Simply accepting the fact that life isn't always fair can go a long way toward helping you relax and feel more positive!

Activity 1: Practice the Steps

Liam and his friend Demarco have been dying to get to the beach, and now Demarco's older brother, Juan, has his license. They come up with a plan to drive to the ocean early Saturday morning, just for the day. Friday night, Demarco calls to say Juan got a last-minute opportunity to go to a concert of his favorite band and has backed out. Liam is really annoyed at the change in plans. He thinks, *This is so unfair!*

What was Liam's off-target thinking error?

_____

_____

> What do you think Liam does (or doesn't do) next as a result of his "It's not fair!" thought?

_____

_____

♡ How do you think Liam feels? (Circle all that apply.)

Sad	Disgusted	Confused	Annoyed
Angry	Worried	Helpless	Anxious
Stressed	Irritable	Excited	Disappointed
Uncomfortable	Rejected	Gloomy	Shaky
Panicked	Frustrated	Miserable	Envious
Hurt	Enraged	Furious	Misunderstood
Desperate	Neutral	Bored	Disinterested

Other(s): _____

How do you think his body responds? (Circle all that apply.)

Heart races	Gets shaky	Muscles tense	Throat feels constricted
Breathes rapidly	Feels sluggish	Gets sweaty	Feels cold
Feels tingly	Hands get clammy	Feels numb	Gets headache
Stomach feels queasy	Feels jittery	Neck feels stiff	Face reddens
Eyes roll	Feels fidgety	Feels warm	Mouth feels dry
Hands clench	Jaw tightens	Chest feels tight	Feels strong

Other(s): _____

✔ Reality check: What can Liam say to himself to challenge his off-target thought? Liam is really annoyed that Demarco's brother is backing out of the beach trip. But rather than staying angry, he tries to understand what happened from Juan's point of view. He asks himself, "What are Juan's reasons? What would I do in the same situation?" Write down what Liam can say to himself after considering these questions to challenge his off-target thought.

_____

_____

_____

_____

Liam's helpful thought and action plan: I really wanted to go to the beach. But I get it that Juan really wants to get to that concert—I'd do the same thing if I were in his shoes. Maybe Demarco and I can hang out at the community pool this weekend and go to the beach another time.

The payoff: How do the helpful thought and action plan improve Liam's situation? Consider the impact on his mood, physical sensations, behavior, and relationships.

_____

_____

_____

_____

_____

_____

_____

_____

Can you see the benefit of forgetting about fairness and trying to see the other person's point of view? Try taking these steps yourself.

Activity 2: Change Your Own Thinking Habit

Remember a situation from your life when you thought "It's not fair!" Describe what happened and how your thinking was off-target.

_____

_____

_____

_____

> What did you do (or not do) next as a result of your "It's not fair!" thought?

_____

_____

_____

_____

How did this thought make you feel?

_____

_____

How did your body respond?

_____

_____

✔ Reality check: What could you have said to yourself to challenge your off-target thought? Some possibilities: "Is life always fair or equal? What did the situation look like from the other person's point of view? Were my expectations reasonable in this case?" After considering these questions, write down what you could have said to yourself to challenge the thought.

_____

_____

_____

_____

☁ What is a more realistic, helpful thought you might have had instead?

_____

_____

_____

_____

🚶 Describe your action plan:

_____

_____

_____

_____

🏅 The payoff: How would this helpful thought and action plan have improved your situation? Consider the impact on your mood, physical sensations, behavior, and relationships.

_____

_____

_____

_____

Much as we might like to always be treated equitably, deep down we know from observation that life just doesn't always work that way. Simply accepting that fact is a giant step toward breaking this habit. You stop feeling like a victim when you realize the world doesn't owe you fairness. You begin to understand that you can cope with disappointment. And rather than feeling frustrated and angry, you can look for ways to work toward what you want.

Try It Out: *Switch Shoes!*

Read the following story. Then consider Alex's point of view. Try putting yourself in the shoes of his parents and grandparents. What do you think they're probably thinking? What broader view can you imagine Alex might have after putting himself in their shoes? Write your answers in the spaces provided.

Alex and his brothers have been looking forward to a planned family camping trip to the mountains this summer. They've saved up their money to go to the amusement park near the campground and plan to spend a day learning to fish. But the week before they're set to leave, Alex's grandmother has a heart attack. His mom heads back to her hometown for two weeks to help her mother recuperate and to cook for Alex's frail grandfather. She promises the boys that they'll take the family trip over spring break instead. Alex wants his father to take them camping without her, but his dad agrees that they'll wait until spring.

Alex's point of view: "My father could take us—he's just being unreasonable!"

Imagine Alex's mother's point of view. What's she thinking?

_____

_____

Imagine Alex's grandmother's point of view. What's she thinking?

_____

_____

Imagine Alex's grandfather's point of view. What's he thinking?

_____

_____

Imagine Alex's father's point of view. What's he thinking?

_____

_____

Now imagine what Alex thinks after he puts himself in all these shoes!

_____

_____

Being able to put yourself in other people's shoes is an important skill to develop even if you don't have any off-target thinking habits. It helps you feel empathy for other people, and make wiser and more considerate decisions.

more for you to do
Learn a Bonus Skill: *Be Grateful!*

As is true with many thinking errors, the "It's not fair!" habit often leads teens to feel like helpless victims. One great way to learn to stop seeing yourself this way and to increase your feelings of contentment is to practice the skill of being grateful. When you feel mistreated, remember how lucky you are in other ways. Often, when you look hard at your disappointments, you can even find a silver lining. Read each of the "It's not fair!" statements below, and then under "However, I'm grateful that …" write what you could feel glad about if you were in each situation. For example, when you're feeling really mad about that 10:00 p.m. curfew, you might write, "However, I'm grateful that my parents care about my safety and how well I do in school."

It's not fair that:	However, I'm grateful that:
My friends didn't agree to my choice of movie!	
My aunt got too busy to take me shopping!	
My brother gets to stay out later than I do!	
We got so much homework over spring break!	
I have to work this summer, and my friends don't!	

Remember how you practiced changing your perspective in chapter 8, when you stepped back and looked at the whole carpet rather than just one corner? Practicing gratitude is a very effective way to change your perspective. Seeing all the angles is especially helpful when your narrow view of what's going on is unrealistic and keeps you from being appreciative of what you have.

the big picture on "it's not fair!" thinking

The automatic habit of expecting fair treatment only makes you unhappy and angry and hurts your relationships because the world simply doesn't work that way. Believing that it ought to leaves you feeling like a victim—and frustrated and angry about being a victim. Once you accept that sometimes things will go your way and sometimes they won't, it becomes possible to react flexibly and problem solve, the hallmarks of a resilient person. And you'll feel a lot happier and calmer when the anger fades away.

Remember:

- Teens with the "It's not fair!" habit get angry and resentful when they feel that they've been unjustly treated, even though fairness is an unrealistic expectation.

- You can break this habit by taking a reality check. Ask yourself: "Is there a good reason for what's happening? Is my point of view the only one?"

- When you stop getting stuck on keeping score, you can begin to be happy for others and generate ideas about what action to take next.

Acknowledgments

This book is based on the principles of cognitive behavior therapy (CBT) and is intended for use with teens. CBT comprises a set of therapeutic approaches that have been demonstrated to improve thoughts, moods, and behaviors. When practiced, they are effective and result in changes in life functioning.

We gratefully acknowledge the foundational work done by B. F. Skinner, Ivan Pavlov, Albert Bandura, Donald Meichenbaum, Albert Ellis, Aaron T. Beck, David Burns, David Barlow, Martin Seligman, and others in the development of CBT. We acknowledge those contributions made by academic researchers and practicing therapists who have enriched the field of CBT, further expanding it, for example, to accommodate behavioral activation and mindfulness.

I, Mary Alvord, wish to offer my sincere appreciation to all the teens who have worked with me over the years. It's been an honor to work with them as they delve into distressing thoughts, feelings, and actions and make efforts to better their lives.

We thank those who have provided feedback in the development of this book—clinicians from Alvord, Baker & Associates including Drs. Lisa Berghorst, Colleen Cummings, Julia Felton, and Veronica Raggi, and to Drs. Dawn Huebner, Karan Lamb, and Bonnie Zucker. Special thanks go to Dr. Anahi Collado and to Melissa Zarger for reading and commenting on the entire document.

Appendix

A Handy List of Challenge Questions

You can download and print a copy of these questions at http://www.newharbinger.com/38891.

The "I Can't" Habit

- What is the evidence that I can't do it?

- What steps can I take to tackle the problem?

- What steps have I taken in the past to learn new skills or tackle other problems?

- Is it possible to ask someone for help?

The Catastrophizing Habit

- How likely is the worst-case scenario?

- Is there any evidence that it's apt to happen?

- What are five other things more likely to happen?

- If something bad does happen, how would I cope?

- What would I tell a friend who had the same thought?

The All-or-Nothing Habit

- Is my thought at one extreme?

- Is there evidence to support my thought?

- Is there evidence against it?

- What are some possibilities that fall in between the extremes?

The Zooming-In-on-the-Negative Habit

- Is there evidence to support my thought?

- Is there evidence against it?

- Am I focusing too much on one detail?

- What good things happened that I'm forgetting?

- Next week, when I think back on today, what will be the most accurate way to remember the big picture?

The "I Should, You Should" Habit

- Were my expectations reasonable in this case?

- What if I substitute "It would be nice if ..." for the should statement?

- How did having a rigid rule help me?

- How did it hurt me?

The Fortune-Telling Habit

- Is my prediction reasonable in this case?

- What evidence do I have to base my fortune-telling on?

- How often am I right when I jump to the conclusion that something bad will happen?

The Mind-Reading Habit

- How do I know for sure what he or she is thinking?

- How do I know it's about me?

- What supports my assumption? What argues against it?

- What are some more likely interpretations of the situation?

- What would I tell a friend who is mind-reading like I just did?

The Blaming Habit

- Am I being fair to myself by taking all the blame?

- Am I being fair to others by blaming them?

- How does blaming myself or someone else help me?

- What are all the factors that may have contributed to this situation?

- Were some or all of these factors beyond anyone's control?

The "It's Not Fair!" Habit

- Is life always fair or equal?

- What did the situation look like from the other person's point of view?

- Were my expectations reasonable in this case?

Resources

Websites

Conquer Negative Thinking for Teens: A Workbook to Break Thought Habits That Are Holding You Back Online

A web page for this book is set up with some accessory materials at http://www .newharbinger.com/38891, including:

- Audio recordings of "Be Mindful of the Moment," a mindfulness meditation, and an "I Can Try!" exercise that addresses the "I can't" habit

- Handouts of the *Nine Thinking Habits* and *A Handy List of Challenge Questions*

- Worksheets illustrating cognitive behavior therapy

Academy of Cognitive Therapy (ACT)

http://www.academyofct.org

ACT supports a web page that provides professionals and parents with book and article resources on assessment and treatment.

American Psychological Association (APA) Annual Stress in America Survey

http://www.stressinamerica.org

The APA has been conducting annual surveys since 2007 measuring stress across the country. The surveys report the leading sources of stress, common behaviors used to manage stress, and the impact of stress on the lives of adults, children, and teens. The connections between mind and body are highlighted. The 2010 and 2013 surveys focus particular attention on teen stress.

American Psychological Association (APA) Psychology Help Center

http://www.apa.org/helpcenter

The APA's help center offers the general public information, tip sheets, and resources on a variety of mental health and mind-body issues.

Anxiety and Depression Association of America (ADAA)

http://www.adaa.org

ADAA is an international organization "dedicated to the prevention, treatment, and cure of anxiety, depressive, obsessive-compulsive, and trauma-related disorders through education, practice, and research." Explore tabs including "Understand the Facts," which contains information on various disorders, and "Live and Thrive," where you will find tips and tools for teens.

Association for Behavioral and Cognitive Therapies (ABCT)

http://www.abct.org

ABCT is an organization committed to investigating and applying evidence-based behavioral, cognitive, and other approaches to treating psychological problems. Two particular sections are of interest: "Get Information" and "Find Help."

Centers for Disease Control and Prevention (CDC)

http://www.cdc.gov/healthyyouth/adolescenthealth/publications.htm

This CDC web page provides a list of publications and other resources focused on adolescent health and mental health.

Centre for Clinical Interventions (CCI)

The CCI is an Australian public health organization that posts various treatment modules. Of particular interest are a series on anxiety and a lesson on behavioral activation.

Mastering your Worries: http://www.cci.health.wa.gov.au/resources/infopax .cfm?Info_ID=46

Behavioral Activation: http://www.cci.health.wa.gov.au/docs/ACFB003.pdf

Substance Abuse and Mental Health Services Administration (SAMHSA)

http://www.samhsa.gov

The Substance Abuse and Mental Health Services Administration (SAMHSA), part of the U.S. Department of Health and Human Services, provides a website with numerous resources and, under the "Find Help & Treatment" tab, hotline numbers and other sources of help.

Apps

CBT Tools for Kids

CBT Tools for Kids is an app for Apple devices that helps teens become more aware of—and better manage—their feelings through the use of cognitive behavior therapy (CBT) skills. Teens monitor their thoughts and emotional states, identify situational triggers, increase their awareness of body sensations, learn how their emotions change over time, and learn to use tools such as relaxation and positive action to manage their thoughts, feelings, and behaviors.

Virtual Hope Box

Though originally designed by the Department of Defense for military personnel and their families, this free app is available to the general public for Apple and Android devices. It's a helpful tool for teens to use to supplement treatment. The app provides relaxation audios, a place to store media that can support you or help lift your mood, positive messages, and coping statements. A clinician's guide and a user's guide are available at http://t2health.dcoe.mil/apps/virtual-hope-box.

CDs and Digital Downloads

Alvord, M. K., B. Zucker, and B. Alvord. *Relaxation and Self-Regulation Techniques for Children and Teens: Mastering the Mind-Body Connection.* Champaign, IL: Research Press, 2011.

This CD offers teens a variety of strategies that can support their efforts to change thought habits. The recordings help listeners increase awareness of their thoughts and physiological reactions to situations. Listeners have the opportunity to practice the skills as they go. Recordings include "Self-Talk" and "Mindfulness," as well as recordings to calm and regulate the mind and body through visualization, progressive muscle relaxation, and calm and attentive breathing. The majority of the scripts are based on cognitive behavior therapy (CBT) and some borrow from Eastern traditions of meditation. The CD tracks are also available as individual digital downloads from Amazon and iTunes.

Alvord, M. K., B. Zucker, and B. Alvord. *Relaxation and Wellness Techniques: Mastering the Mind-Body Connection.* Champaign, IL: Research Press, 2013.

This CD is a helpful resource to support the efforts of noticing and making changes to thinking habits. Targeted toward older teens and adults, this CD provides ten recordings with CBT techniques and meditative tracks to help achieve a sense of calm and quiet the mind. For example, a recording titled "Challenging Your Catastrophic Thoughts" specifically addresses anxious "what if" thinking and leads the listener through the process of questioning the unhelpful thoughts. Visualization, progressive muscle relaxation, breathing approaches, mindfulness, and Eastern meditation practices round out the CD, which is also available for download from Amazon and iTunes.

Further Reading

Antony, M., and R. Swinson. *Shyness and Social Anxiety Workbook: Proven, Step-by-Step Techniques for Overcoming Your Fear.* Oakland, CA: New Harbinger Publications, 2008.

———. *When Perfect Isn't Good Enough: Strategies for Coping with Perfectionism.* Oakland, CA: New Harbinger Publications, 2008.

Burns, D. D. *Feeling Good: The New Mood Therapy.* New York: HarperCollins Publishers, 2008.

Duckworth, A. *Grit: The Power of Passion and Perseverance.* New York: Scribner, 2016.

Dweck, C. *Mindset: The New Psychology of Success.* New York: Ballantine Books, 2006.

Vo, D. Z. *The Mindful Teen: Powerful Skills to Help You Handle Stress One Moment at a Time.* Oakland, CA: New Harbinger Publications, 2015.

Mary Karapetian Alvord, PhD, is a licensed psychologist with more than thirty-five years of clinical experience, and is director of Alvord, Baker & Associates. She specializes in treating children, adolescents, and adults using cognitive behavior therapies. A central focus is children and teens with depression, anxiety disorders, attention deficit/hyperactivity disorder (ADHD), and other emotional and behavioral regulation problems. She is adjunct associate professor of psychiatry and behavioral sciences at The George Washington University School of Medicine and Health Sciences, and is a fellow of both the American Psychological Association and of the Association for Behavioral and Cognitive Therapies. She is coauthor of *Resilience Builder Program* and the audio recordings, *Relaxation and Self-Regulation Techniques for Children and Teens* and *Relaxation and Wellness Techniques* (for adults).

Anne McGrath, MA, is executive editor of publications at *U.S. News & World Report*, where she has written and edited on subjects from health and mental health to investing and education for over thirty years. She is currently responsible for three of the publisher's signature guidebooks: *Best Graduate Schools, Best Colleges,* and *Best Hospitals*. She is also original editor of several books on getting into law school and medical school. She holds her master's in journalism from Syracuse University.

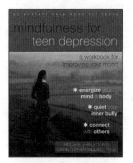

Register your **new harbinger** titles for additional benefits!

When you register your **new harbinger** title—purchased in any format, from any source—you get access to benefits like the following:

- Downloadable accessories like printable worksheets and extra content

- Instructional videos and audio files

- Information about updates, corrections, and new editions

Not every title has accessories, but we're adding new material all the time.

Access free accessories in 3 easy steps:

1. Sign in at NewHarbinger.com (or **register** to create an account).

2. Click on **register a book**. Search for your title and click the **register** button when it appears.

3. Click on the **book cover or title** to go to its details page. Click on **accessories** to view and access files.

That's all there is to it!

If you need help, visit:

NewHarbinger.com/accessories

new harbinger
CELEBRATING
40 YEARS